THE PSYCHOLOGICAL ELEMENT IN THE ENGLISH SOCIOLOGICAL NOVEL OF THE NINETEENTH CENTURY

THE PSYCHOLOGICAL ELEMENT IN THE ENGLISH SOCIOLOGICAL NOVEL OF THE NINETEENTH CENTURY

SIJNA DE VOOYS

HASKELL HOUSE
Publishers of Scholarly Books
NEW YORK
1966

published by

HASKELL HOUSE

Publishers of Scholarly Books

30 East 10th Street • New York, N. Y. 10003

PRINTED IN UNITED STATES OF AMERICA

0838305393

CONTENTS

General Introduction

The object of every story-teller is to make his audience listen with rapt attention, so that for the time being they forget the where and when of their own existence and live the life of the fictitious persons with whose sorrows they sympathize and in whose joys they rejoice, whose adventures they follow, whose world they believe in. What story-teller who has felt the glory of his power to take his hearers with him to the fairy-land of his fantasy, who has seen in their eyes the surrender, who has heard the silence about him, has not been conscious of the longing to leave an impression behind in their minds that may outlast the moment of absorption, — of the wish to give them what he has found as the greatest thing in life, his sincerest convictions, his best thoughts, his warmest feelings? It is thus that the teacher awakes in the story-teller. He is no longer content with amusing his hearers by giving some colour to the grey monotony of their every-day existence, but he tries to penetrate to their innermost being and to make them look with his eyes.

Just as it is with the story-teller of our days, so it was at the beginning of English prose fiction; the writers of romances considered it as their chief object to amuse their readers, to make them follow the hero through a series of wonderful adventures, or as we find in Caxton's Prologue to Sir Thomas Malory's *Morte d'Arthur* (1485): "And for to pass the time, this book shall be pleasant to read in"; still, underlying the idea of giving pleasure, there is the wish to excite admiration for the courage of the hero in fighting his enemies, or for his fortitude in adversity and to raise the longing to imitate him, to take him as an example.

So we see that the didactic element can be traced already in the mediaeval romance, which gives, as Professor Stoddard[1] puts it: "heroic types, ideal personages in the armor of knights"; but the wish to teach is more than vaguely discernible from the beginning in the English novel.

I agree with Professor Saintsbury[2] that it will not do to draw the line of separation between romance and novel as: "the story of incident and the story of character and motive", but that "the real principle and essence of the novel as distinguished from the romance is its connection with actual ordinary life; still I think that Professor Stoddard hits upon the real distinction in bringing home to us that where there is no individual life presented to us, there is no real novel.

If then the novelist gets hold of his readers' attention and succeeds in making them see the personality of his hero, this is of the greatest importance for the sociological novel[3], because "things seen are mightier than things heard."

The facts given in the sociological novel we have all heard and read of. The great thinkers have put them down in statistics which lay bare the facts and make us understand how wide the gulf is between rich and poor, how vast the number of the paupers and the unemployed, but these facts are like a sad account of things far off that we listen to without emotion, because the persons are unknown to us; we understand, but our feelings are not stirred.

The novelists, who are the feelers, ask our sympathy for a few out of that vast number, perhaps one or two whom

[1] Cf. A. F. H. Stoddard, *The Evolution of the English Novel,* Ch. II, p. 47.
[2] Cf. George Saintsbury, *The English Novel,* Ch. I, p. 8. Ch. IV, p. 154.
[3] For a definition of the sociological novel cf. L. Cazamian, *Le Roman Social en Angleterre,* Introduction, III, p. 11.

we see before our eyes, whose acquaintance we make, whose struggles we realize, whose misery touches us, because we not only hear the facts, but we see them by the light that the author throws on them, as now and then we look into the inner being of a friend in a quiet hour of revelation.

Understanding and sympathy are the two great forces that shall move the world onward; the knowing is the first spark, it is the feeling that fans it into a bright, purifying flame.

The more the characters appeal to us, the better we shall realize them and see, not only how they are living and what they are doing, but what they live for and why they leave so many things undone.

And if this is true for the psychological novel, it is the more so for the sociological novel, because here the author's intention is not to give a better insight into the characters and consequently into the living beings about us, but his aim is to stir the fire of sympathy in us, to keep it burning, to prevent us from taking life the easier, the better, from going on like a horse with blinkers on, seeing straight before us nothing but our own interest as the be-all and end-all of life.

In this way the sociological novel will prepare the ground for the doers, the social reformers.

The fundamental idea that we find expressed in the sociological novel is: "Life is not what it ought to be". This thought returns again and again in various forms and though it is impossible to draw a sharp line, yet we find here as everywhere in literature, the two ruling ideas: romanticism and realism. In order to show that life is not what it ought to be, romanticism will give us life as it might be, an existence so pure and good in itself that as H. G. Wells tells us in his novel *Men like Gods* the wish of the Earthling: "Good morning" is answered by an astonished "Why not?" from the Utopian.

Romanticism [1] on the wings of fantasy flies high over the world with its great sorrows, and its little daily cares, raising the longing to reach such an ideal state, but at the same time giving a sharp criticism of existing conditions by the comparisons between the attitude of life on Earth and in Utopia.

Realism on the other hand gives us a faithful picture of the facts of actual life, showing in glaring colours or in sombre tints the squalid misery, the injustice, the emptiness of the world in general or of a special class of people. Such a picture stirs the emotions and makes us aware that we have been day-dreaming in our own little world; it rouses us, opens our eyes, and awakes our inner consciousness to the question: "If things are as bad as that, are not we too responsible?"

In treating this subject I want to state at the outset that I am obliged to put some limits and therefore have excluded the novel in which the Romantic view comes more to the fore, i. e. the fantastic or Utopian novel, as well as the purely political novel, choosing as a subject for discussion the realistic sociological novel of the nineteenth century, especially those treating the evils of the whole social system.

It is curious to consider that we cannot find a continued line of development in the English sociological novel, but that we notice three distinct periods:

I The Sociological Novel influenced by the French Revolution. 1790-1800

II The Sociological Novel influenced by the Industrial Revolution. 1830-1866

III The Sociological Novel influenced by the Rise of Democracy. 1880-1900

[1] Cf. Leslie Stephen, *English Literature and Society in the Eighteenth Century*, Ch. V, p. 212.

These periods distinguished by the ideas which give them a character of their own, are still bound together by the leading thoughts:

a. Dissatisfaction with the existing conditions.

b. A longing to return to Nature.

c. The necessity of simplification as regards social life.

Though the first period chronologically does not strictly belong to the nineteenth century, it will be impossible to omit it, because in bringing to the fore the psychological element in the sociological novel of the nineteenth century, it will be necessary to look backwards to the last decade of the eighteenth century.

Introduction to Chapter I

The Ideas of the first Period: The Sociological Novel influenced by the French Revolution

In speaking of the influence of the French Revolution we should be careful not to be misled by the supposition that the French Revolution was the power that created the principle of reliance on truth and reason which characterizes the above-mentioned period, but rather consider the French Revolution as the quickening influence that roused the contemplating minds to activity for, as Walter Raleigh [1] expresses it: "Towards the end of the eighteenth century theory was rife in England."

The warning, Leslie Stephen [2] gives with respect to the political movements at the end of the eighteenth century in England is equally true for the literature of that time:

"It has been easy to ascribe to the contagion of French example political movements which were already beginning in England and which were modified rather than materially altered by our share in the great European convulsion"; and that the rational tendency was the mental attitude of the great thinkers earlier in the eighteenth century we find expressed by L. Cazamian [3]:

"Vers le milieu du XVIIIe siècle, le rythme psychologique de la pensée anglaise, d'accord avec le rythme européen,

[1] Walter Raleigh, *The English Novel,* Ch. VIII, p. 238.

[2] Leslie Stephen, *The English Utilitarians,* Vol. I, Ch. III : V, p. 121.

[3] L. Cazamian, *L'Angleterre Moderne,* Ch. II, p. 38.

accuse une prédominance incontestée des facultés intellectuelles sur les facultés sensitives.

Tous ces éléments trouvent leur synthèse dans la grande poussée de rationalisme spéculatif et pratique qu'on appelle le mouvement utilitaire."

And in tracing back still further we find that as early as 1640 John Locke had made it clear that truth and reason are the best guides to justice; his two main characteristics [1] were first his craving to know and to speak the truth and the whole truth in everything, truth not for a purpose, but for itself and secondly his perfect trust in Reason as the guide, the only guide to truth.

In his *Essay concerning Humane Understanding* [2] (1640) he wrote:

"He who has raised himself above the Alms-Basket, and not content to live lazily on scraps of begged Opinions, sets his own Thoughts on work, to find and follow Truth, will (whatever he lights on) not miss the Hunter's satisfaction; every moment of his Pursuit will reward his Pains with some Delight, and he will have Reason to think his time not ill spent, even when he cannot much boast of any great acquisition."

Whereas here Locke considers Truth as the aim of man, he points out that Reason is the guide to lead us to that aim:

"In all Things therefore where we have clear Evidence from our Ideas, and those Principles of Knowledge, I have above mentioned, Reason is the proper Judge" [3].

Locke's disciple, Rousseau, added to the principle of reliance on truth and reason the idea that it is urgently necess-

1 Cf. R. H. Quick, *Educational Reformers,* Ch. XIII, p. 220.

2 J. Locke, *Essay concerning Humane Understanding,* cf. Epistle to the Reader.

3 J. Locke, Book IV, Ch. XVIII, p. 351. cf. also: p. 341.

ary to follow the teaching of nature in order to find happiness.

In his *Emile*[1] he says: "Observez la nature et suivez la route qu'elle trace," and later on: "Au contraire, plus l'homme est resté près de sa condition naturelle, plus la différence de ses facultés à ses désirs est petite et moins par conséquent il est éloigné d'être heureux"[2].

Rousseau, however, does not consider Reason and Nature as all sufficient, for more than once he insists on the necessity of obeying the dictates of the heart: "Je ferois voir que justice et bonté ne sont point seulement des mots abstraits, de purs êtres moraux formés par l'entendement; mais de véritables affections de l'âme éclairée par la raison et qui ne sont qu'un progrès ordonné de nos affections primitives; que par la raison seule, indépendamment de la conscience, on ne peut établir aucune loi naturelle et que tout le droit de la Nature n'est qu'un chimère, s'il n'est fondé sur un besoin naturel du coeur humain[3].

Or again: „L'homme qui a le plus vécu n'est pas celui qui a compté le plus d'années, mais celui qui a le plus senti la vie"[4].

The influence of Rousseau is clearly to be seen in the sociological novel in the last decade of the eighteenth century, and though the thought that feeling is not a negligible quantity, is often expressed by Godwin and his contemporaries, still I agree with L. Cazamian[5], who, in giving the first place to the emotions says:

[1] I quote from: *Emile ou de l'Education* par J. J. Rousseau, 1762. Amsterdam, Tome I, Livre I, p. 57.

[2] id., Tome I, Livre II, p. 155.

[3] id., Tome II, Livre IV, p. 263.

[4] id., Tome I, Livre I, p. 21.

[5] L. Cazamian, *L'Evolution Psychologique et la Littérature en Angleterre,* Ch. VII. p. 159.

„Rien ne pouvait mieux achever la préparation morale commencée depuis un siècle que cette expérience des grandes émotions collectives", but still concludes that reason was the all-conquering force: „La contagion révolutionnaire est rationnelle autant et plus que sentimentale; c'est au nom de la raison, par des argumentations passionnées, que se livre sur le sol anglais la grande bataille d'idées" [1].

It has often been pointed out [2] that the French Revolution aroused in England a conflict of opinions of which it is not easy to say which party had the ascendancy, but we can safely say that the French Revolution strengthened the rational tendencies that prevailed in England in the eighteenth century.

Truth and Reason were the guides that led Thomas Paine and William Godwin, the foremost propagators of revolutionary thought [3] in England, to Liberty, to Natural Equality, and the Rights of Man.

The work of Thomas Paine: *Rights of Man* appeared in 1797, but in 1795 he wrote in the Preface:

"Man will herein find all his natural, civil and divine rights more perfectly and rationally defined than he was aware of, and will feel his reason roused into action, and himself animated in the universal cause of human nature, with that fervour which springs alone from reflection and a sense of conscious right. He will look back at the iron rod of assumption and despotism with horror, and revolt at the recollection of the impositions he has suffered himself to be deceived into by the artifices of the designing and venal few."

Insisting on the Rights of Man, he emphasized the dissatis-

[1] id., p. 160.
[2] Cf. Leslie Stephen, *The English Utilitarians,* Vol I, Ch. III, Social Problems.
Cf. Leslie Stephen, *English Literature and Society in the Eighteenth Century,* Ch. V, p. 181.

faction with the existing conditions; for him it was not as with Rousseau the Return to Nature which would inevitably lead to happiness, but the adherence to Truth, or, as he expresses it: "Truth is the fountain of happiness, the harbinger of freedom, the basis of justice, and the source of judgment. It is the birthright of nature and the germ of felicity."

In the same spirit of enthusiasm William Godwin, of whom I shall have occasion to speak more in detail in Chapter I, wrote in a letter to Sheridan [1]: "Give to a state but liberty enough, and it is impossible that vice should exist in it."

About that enthusiasm Mr. H. P. G. Quack [2] says calmly and soberly: „Men wond zich op. Men dacht in gemoede dat men het begin van een duizendjarig rijk van vrede en liefde zou gaan beleven. In die stemming verkeerde ook de anders zoo koele en onaandoenlijke William Godwin."

Truth, Liberty, and Return to Nature were the watchwords of these enthusiasts, but, as Leslie Stephen has pointed out, the cry: 'Return to Nature' has been interpreted in different ways; with the revolutionists it means "the demand for a thorough-going reconstruction of the whole philosophical and social fabric" [3].

In this way the cry: 'Return to Nature' is closely connected with the first leading thought in the sociological novel of the first Period:

Dissatisfaction with the existing conditions; the general doctrine of the rights of Man that all men are by nature free and equal, covers the doctrine that the inequality and despotism of the existing order are hateful.

The Return to Nature, which is the second leading thought,

[1] Cf. Kegan Paul, *William Godwin*, Vol. I, Ch. III, p. 76.

[2] *De Socialisten, Personen en Stelsels*, 2e druk, Ch. XIII, p. 511.

[3] Leslie Stephen, *English Literature and Society in the Eighteenth Century*, Ch. V, p. 220.

also includes the glorification of the natural man, which, though not quite a new idea in English Literature [1], still, under the influence of Rousseau [2] had come to new life, and is expressed as the third leading thought: the necessity of simplification as regards social life in the disdain for rank, the praise of independence of mind and the glorification of the country-gentleman.

[1] Cf. Aphra Behn, *Oroonoko,* (1913) pp. 4-9, and Sarah Fielding, *David Simple.*

[2] Cf. *Emile,* Tome I, Livre I, p. 10. Cf. *Emile,* Tome II, Livre II, p. 51.

CHAPTER I

The Sociological Novel, influenced by the French Revolution

Godwin and his contemparies: Thomas Holcroft, Robert Bage, Charlotte Smith, and Charles Lloyd.

The sociological novel of this period is usually called the Revolutionary Novel and though this name is slightly misleading, because one is apt to think of a novel, advocating revolution, it will serve our purpose to use the term, provided we keep in mind the conclusion laid down in the Introduction to Chapter I about the influence of the French Revolution.

When we look back to the period of the Revolutionary School, it seems strange at first sight that of the novels written by the authors of the last decade of the eighteenth century only one [1] has survived, but when we examine more closely some of the principal productions:

Anna St. Ives (1792) by Thomas Holcroft,
Man as he is (1792) by Robert Bage,
The Banished Man (1794) by Charlotte Smith,
Edmund Oliver (1798) by Charles Lloyd,

we shall see that time has dealt justly with them in suffering them to sink into oblivion.

Without doubt these novels are highly interesting, when considered from an historical point of view, and therefore of great importance for our present purpose, because they

[1] *Caleb Williams* (1794) by William Godwin, reprinted 1903 in the series: Half-forgotten Books, Routledge.

form as it were the background against which Godwin as a novelist stands out. The fact that Holcroft's *Hugh Trevor* appeared later than *Caleb Williams*, has led me to omit *Hugh Trevor*, which, though begun in 1794 was not finished before 1797; for the same reason Bage's *Hermsprong* (1796) can be passed over, but *Edmund Oliver* by Ch. Lloyd (1798) cannot be spared, because, though chronologically the last, it was written to refute Godwin's principles.

I hope I shall succeed in pointing out in the following pages that it is the psychological element in Godwin's *Caleb Williams* which forms its saving quality.

This element is sadly wanting in the other novels mentioned above; the "natural man" becomes highly unnatural, being an image of perfection, a mouthpiece of revolutionary ideas, and therefore rather a type than a personality.

The sociological novel will only have a chance of being a living force, when the hero is not an oracle formulating the thoughts and opinions of his time, but a "struggling, erring human being" [1] who asks for our understanding and our sympathy.

Thomas Holcroft has the credit of having inspired Godwin. As Godwin says himself: "The four principal oral instructors to whom I feel my mind indebted for improvement were Joseph Fawcet, Thomas Holcroft, George Dyson and Samuel Taylor Coleridge [2] — We find Holcroft's views expressed in his novel *Anna St. Ives*, or, as W. Cross [3] says: "the whole revolutionary programme presented in the pages of one novel."

In his *Political Justice* Godwin has worked out the following principles:

that true happiness should be founded on a sense of justice

[1] G. Eliot.

[2] Kegan Paul, *William Godwin*, Ch. II, p. 26.

[3] W. Cross, *The Development of the English Novel*, Ch. III, p. 89.

and on equality, though not a clockwork uniformity for all men, the conviction that there should be no property, that alle selfishness should be done away with, that there should be no constraint or law, and therefore no marriage, and that Reason will lead to a state of voluntary deeds and of pleasure and pride in work.

Godwin himself expresses it in the following way:

"The equality for which we are pleading is an equality that would succeed to a state of great intellectual improvement."

"The institution of marriage is a system of fraud and men who carefully mislead their judgments in the daily affair of their life, must always have a crippled judgment in every other concern."

"It is only a calm and clear conviction of justice, of justice mutually to be rendered and received, of happiness to be produced by the desertion of our most rooted habits, that can introduce an invariable system of this sort."

"It is true that the proper method of curing this inequality is by reason and not by violence" [1].

We shall see that the same ideas: equality, no property, no selfishness, no marriage, and reliance on Reason, are proclaimed by Holcroft's hero in *Anna St. Ives*, Frank Henley "the natural man," pleading: "What is rank? Does it imply superiority of mind? Or is there any other superiority? Am I not a man? And who is more? Have the titled earned their dignities by any proof of exalted virtue? Were not these dignities things of accident, in which the owners had no share and of which they are generally unworthy?" [2]

Frank's imagination, warm with the sublimity of his subject, drew "a bold and splendid picture of the felicity of

[1] *Political Justice*, Book VIII, Ch. VI, pp. 58-70.

[2] *Anna St. Ives*, Vol. II, Letter 39, p. 219.

that state of society, when personal property no longer shall exist, when the whole torrent of mind shall unite in enquiry after the beautiful and the true, when it shall no longer be diverted by those insignificant pursuits to which the absurd follies that originate in our false wants give birth, when individual selfishness shall be unknown and when all shall labour for the good of all."

"Of all the regulations which were ever suggested to the mistaken tyranny of selfishness, none perhaps to this day have surpassed the despotism of those which undertake to bind not only body to body but soul to soul, to all futurity, in despite of every possible change which our virtues and our vices might effect" [1].

"All should be under the command of reason, other commands are tyranny. Reason and not relationship alone can give authority" [2].

When we consider *Anna St. Ives* apart from the revolutionary ideas propagated by the hero, we find a conventional, sentimental novel, written in letters. Anna Wenbourne St. Ives writes to her bosom friend Louisa Clifton about her two lovers, Frank Henley, a perfect young man of low birth, whose character is all nobleness, as Anna writes: "He overlooks no living creature, to whom he can give aid. He loses no opportunity of gaining the esteem and affection of high and low, rich and poor. His delicacy never slumbers. His thirst of doing good is never assuaged. I am young it is true, but I never before met a youth so deserving" [3] and Coke Clifton, a man of the world with perfect manners and a wicked heart.

Frank writes to his friend Oliver Trenchard about his struggle to give up Anna, whereas Coke Clifton writes to

[1] *Anna St. Ives,* Vol. V, Letter 27, pp. 32-36.
[2] id., Vol. IV, Letter 79, pp. 228-230.
[3] id., Vol. II, Letter 20, p. 28.

Guy Fairfax at Venice about his good luck in having met a beautiful girl with advanced ideas about marriage.

It goes without saying that Frank Henley always comes to the rescue in the nick of time to save his beloved from death and dishonour, but it is typical for the spirit of the book that it does not finish up with the reward Frank gets in Anna's love. Anna mentions by the way in Vol. VII, Letter 128, that the marriage will take place in a month, buth the real ending [1] is a full account of the way in which Frank Henley converts the reprobate Coke Clifton by reasoning; so much so, that the villain, overcome by remorse calls his rival a "surgeon for the mind" and enthusiastically exclaims: "The soul of benevolence, of tenderness, of attention, of love, of all the divine faculties that make men deities, infuses itself and pervades you."

And when he is attacked by doubt and cannot yet believe in the new-found happiness, saying:

"You would realize the fable of Pygmalion and would infuse soul into marble!", Frank, like a forgiving God, assures him: "There is no need; you have a soul already; inventive, capacious, munificent, sublime!"

To give an idea of the sentimental tone of the book it will be sufficient to mention the episode of the goldfinch [2] "King Pepin". Anna could not live in Paris without her goldfinch, her dear Louisa's gift, but in her hurry she leaves it behind, and on finding this out, accuses herself of the basest ingratitude, but oh! the exquisite joy at young Mr. Henley coming up full speed on the bay mare, bringing her charming favourite!

Here and there we meet some relieving touches in the contemplation of Nature. We cannot help thinking that the

[1] *Anna St. Ives,* Vol. V, Letter 130.
[2] id., Vol. I, Letter I, p. 9.

following words might equally well apply to our time with its rushing automobiles and motorbuses: "Nothing, except the inordinate ardour of the mind to enjoy, could induce people on a journey of pleasure to hurry, as they do, through villages, towns, and countries, pass unnoticed the most magnificent buildings, and the most delightful prospects that forests, rivers, and mountains can afford, and wilfully exclude themselves from all the riches of nature. And if so, a portable closet, or rather a flying watchbox, is but a blundering contrivance" [1].

Robert Bage, whose novel *Man as he is*, appeared in the same year as *Anna St. Ives*, possessed a quality, very rare in writers of sociological novels, namely a sense of humour. This prevents him from sentimentalizing and enables him to make his characters more human than those we meet in *Anna St. Ives* [2].

In the very first chapter he tells us that Lady Mary Paradyne had little fortune and was therefore under the necessity of setting a very high value upon rank. In this way he puts in his principles about equality and justice without preaching, for instance when he says: "The Earl of Auschamp cannot make Sir George comprehend that great political truth that power is always right", but even Bage cannot let the opportunity pass by of inserting the opinion of an unnamed old friend who is enthusiastically looking forward to the coming glory of the age of truth and reason. "The age of chivalry, heaven be praised, is gone" [1]. Instead of generous loyalty to rank there will be an attachment to peace, to law, to the general happiness of mankind, instead

[1] Vol. I, *Anna St. Ives.*
[2] Cf. Saintsbury, *The English Novel*, Ch. IV, p. 164.
[3] Robert Bage, *Man as he is*, Vol. IV, Ch. 93, p. 73.

of submission an unassuming consciousness of natural equality and an honest veneration of superior talents.

Like the other writers of the Revolutionary School Bage was strongly under the influence of Rousseau. He begins his Preface by mentioning his name. "To a refined and sensible people, says Mr. Rousseau, instruction can only be offered in form of a novel", but this influence is especially to be seen in his adherence to the teaching of nature, in his belief in the power of education, and in the fact that he contrasts the tyranny of the passions which makes Sir George Paradyne a slave to selfish pleasures, with the calm influence of reason, which prevents Miss Colerain from yielding to the longing of her heart. About education he says: "Mothers sow the seeds of vanity in their daughters' minds. So Parents give their offspring a thousand wants which nature never gave" [1].

The first of the leading motives: 'Dissatisfaction with the existing conditions' Bage gives in the title: "Man as he is", which he explains later on:

"When I consider what man might be, I am sorry to see him as he is" [2], and the third motive: 'Simplification,' in the character of Mr. Lindsay, the tutor, who in spite of poverty and misfortune keeps his independent spirit and, when he is offered a Government post refuses saying: "I cannot accept of bread with the condition annexed of no longer daring to think for myself" [3], and in the character of Mr. James Paradyne, a plain country gentleman without prejudices who thinks that "looking at other people's estates is not so good as cultivating one's own" [4].

The story tells how Sir George Paradyne, liberating him-

[1] Robert Bage, *Man as he is*, Vol. I, Ch. 9, pp. 78, 80.
[2] id., Vol. IV, Ch. 29.
[3] id., Vol. I, Ch. 6, p. 50.
[4] id., Vol. I, Ch. 8, p. 65.

self from the influence of his mother, goes with a tutor, Mr. Lindsay on a tour through Great Britain, and meets Miss Colerain, who is ruined by a rejected suitor. She is a girl, considered as singular, of an independent mind; as her friend says: "She was not content with disregarding fashion, she disregarded fashionable folks also, she neglected the routine of visits, loved books better than cards, besides she had the humour of owing obligation to nobody. She never was so happy as when she was buried alive on Combor heath."

Sir George is deeply impressed by Miss Colerain's beauty and character and Miss Colerain is grateful, when he buys the White House, so that she can stay in her home and is pleased with his visits up to the moment when he becomes too free of speech.

Then she leaves the White House and tries to forget him, as she cannot love a man whom she does not respect. Sir George goes on the grand tour and tries to find comfort first in the company of Lady Ann Brixton, an heiress and later on in Paris, where he is "floating on the sea of folly". He is on the point of losing his reputation as well as his fortune, but after many adventures the thought of Miss Colerain saves him. He comes back to the White House full of remembrances; in his melancholy he believes death to be near and writes his last will, but, though still sore and embittered, he is encouraged by the sympathy of his sister who writes to him: "The book of nature still lies open before you. In labouring for the happiness of man, you would certainly find your own" [1].

She brings about a reunion with Miss Colerain, and however much Sir George has protested: "I will be no man's slave and

[1] Robert Bage, *Man as he is*, Vol. IV, Ch. 112, p. 197.

no man's property. That lesson at least I learned in France" [1], he submits to the yoke of love.

The story is interrupted every now and then by episodes, the most important of them being that of Miss Zapora, a beautiful pilgrim and that of Fidel, the black servant; these episodes are not connected with the experiences of Sir George, but are merely put in to illustrate the hatred of tyranny, thus being related in spirit only.

The tone of *The Banished Man* by Charlotte Smith is quite different; it was written two years later (July 30. 1794), in the Avis au Lecteur, prefacing the second volume the author writes in a note: "I had not then heard of or seen a work called: "Things as they are", from which we may conclude that this Avis was written a short time only after Godwin's *Things as they are,* or *the Adventures of Caleb Williams.* Charlotte Smith writes in the Preface to Volume I: "Formerly I rejoiced at the probability of freedom in France; now I think that Englishmen must execrate the abuse of the name of Liberty that followed."

In giving a picture of the sad realities of war and the miserable state of the refugees she confesses that she has lost all her confidence in the glory that was to come, she hates tyranny just as much as Robert Bage does, but she considers the freedom now attained in France more tyrannical than the laws of the past.

Her hero, the Chevalier d'Alonville, realized all the evils, brought about by the Republican army and "his heart sunk in reflecting on the sad condition to which so many brave men were reduced and the deplorable state of the country from whence they were driven, for no other crime than adherence to the king whom they had sworn to defend; and

[1] Robert Bage, *Man as he is,* Vol. IV, Ch. 27, p. 154.

to a government which, however defective, was infinitely preferable to the tyrannical anarchy which had, under the pretence of curing those defects, brought an everlasting disgrace on the French name"[1].

And the author herself thinks that it is not necessary any longer to look for new Gothic horrors, when the real horrors in France exceed them all; she calls France "a country where murder stalks abroad and calls itself patriotism; where the establishment of liberty serves as a pretence for the violation of humanity"[2], but she distinguishes very clearly the sense of freedom in France and the true English principles: a hatred of tyranny and injustice under whatever semblance they appear.

Ellesmere, the Englishman, gives his opinion to d'Allonville, the emigrant, in the following words: "I as an Englishman, deplore the injury done to the cause of rational liberty throughout the world, I deplore, as a citizen of that world, the general devastation, the blood that has been shed in the field, or on the scaffold, and the stupendous destruction that has overwhelmed a great nation"[3]. So we see that fundamentally Charlotte Smith is at one with Holcroft and Bage, but for one point of difference: she does not believe in Reason as a never erring guide. The end of Volume IV[4], which we may consider as the moral of the story, gives the reflections of d'Alonville, the Banished Man:

"What I now possess, is less the effect of reflection and reason, than of the harsh lessons I have received in the school of adversity."

The story tells that at the time when the French were

[1] *The Banished Man,* Vol. I, Ch. 9, p. 175.
[2] id., Vol. II, *Avis au Lecteur,* VI.
[3] id., Vol. IV, Ch. 13, p. 322.
[4] id., Vol. IV, Ch. 13, p. 339.

following the Austrian and Russian troops in their retreat, a wounded French nobleman and his son, the Chevalier d'Alonville, are hospitably received at the castle of Rosenheim. The Chevalier has many opportunities of assisting the Baroness and her daughter, but is estranged from them by the calummy of the almoner Heurthofen. Here we meet the same contrast as in the above-mentioned novels: the contrast between simple honesty and scheming hypocrisy.

The Chevalier meets another refugee, De Touranges, and accompanies him to Berlin, Vienna, and at last to Prague, where they meet two Englishmen. D'Alonville makes friends with one of them, Ellesmere, who falls in love with Alexina, a Polish exile; together they go to England, where by chance they find the relations of De Touranges. Madame de Touranges introduces d'Alonville to a young friend, Miss Denzil, a girl of seventeen, not perfectly handsome, but the most interesting he has ever seen. Miss Denzil pities the banished man and her natural, candid simplicity soon gets the better of artificial reserve. Her mother [1] is a poor author who works for her children. Angelina Denzil prefers the poor emigrant to a rich lover.

The Chevalier is induced by a friend to go to France in disguise. In travelling through the Northern provinces of France he cannot help exclaiming bitterly: "And these are the boasted blessings of that liberty for which they have been four years contending — infatuated, misled people [2].

After terrible experiences in the Castle of Vaudrecour, full of Gothic horrors, he is taken prisoner, condemned by his own brother and his old enemy, Heurthofen. His brother wants to convert him, but the Chevalier is repulsed by the Republican

[1] In the person of Mrs. Denzil, Charlotte Smith has given a picture of her own life.

[2] *The Banished Man,* Vol. II, Ch. 5, p. 91.

ideas. He is sent to England with valuable effects, belonging to his brother.

On coming back to England he finds Angelina in deep sorrow about her mother's illness and in great anxieties about pecuniary difficulties; he is able now to pay off the debts, he marries Angelina, but has to accept the post of tutor of Lord Aberdore's sons and is obliged to keep his marriage a secret. He is suspected of being a spy, but gets into Lord Aberdore's good graces by his brave activity during a fire. Mrs. Denzil proves to be a relation of Lady Aberdore's and all difficulties are removed.

The Banished Man and his wife form the plan to leave England and to go to Vienna, where they find a small, but pleasant home. Ellesmere, who has married the Polish exile and by this has incurred the displeasure of his relations, writes to him: "As well as I love England, I can be content to quit it, if the luxuries, that are here accounted among the necessaries of a man of family, cannot be enjoyed but at the expence of that independence" [1].

The Banished Man as well as his English friend is happy in the conclusion: "In losing every thing but my honour and my integrity, I have learned that he who retains those qualities, can never be degraded, however humble may be his fortune" [2].

The plot of *The Banished Man* is more elaborate than that of the novels discussed above, and there is an attempt at characterization; still there is hardly any analysis of personality.

Whereas in this novel Independence of Mind comes most to the fore, the Return to Nature and the Simplification of life are the leading motives in *Edmund Oliver* by Charles Lloyd (1798). The Return to Nature appears here in the form of

[1] *The Banished Man,* Vol. IV, Ch. 13, p. 327.
id., p. 340.

the praise of country-life and the contempt of cities: "Cities are the very graves, the cemetries of human virtue! Sincerity, simplicity of heart, genius and purity of principle, all necessarily die away in them" [1].

The unnatural flocking together of the species hardens and unsocializes the heart more perhaps than uniform solitude" [2].

The "natural man" in this novel is Charles Maurice, who preaches to Edmund Oliver: "Human wants are few, and I deem it criminal, indeed an actual robbery to devote more to myself or family than would fall to our share, were property equalized" [3], and Edmund Oliver sees the cure for unhappiness and lack of purpose in life in unselfishness, simplification, and intellectual pursuit: "We are all unhappy, all complaining, all friendless; all lamenting the want of an object in life! When, if we would but annihilate selfishness, regard the interests of others as our own, narrow our physical sphere, and widen our intellectual one, we might be happy at all times" [4].

Charles Lloyd explains the purpose of his book, which he inscribes to his friend Charles Lamb, in the Advertisement. He sees a great danger in the rejection of cohabitation and in a note he refers to Godwin's essay on this subject in the Enquirer, because "it would lead to a mad spirit of experiment that would eradicate all the valuable feelings of man's nature." He believes that "domestic connections which are only coeval with the existence of marriage, are the necessary means of disciplining Beings, at first merely sentient, to a rational and enlarged benevolence."

The hero, Edmund Oliver, deprived of his inheritance by scheming nephews, filled with a sense of his own unworthiness,

[1] *Edmund Oliver,* Vol. I, Letter 7, p. 102.

[2] id., Vol. I, Letter 17, p. 101.

[3] id., Vol. II, Letter 52, p. 52.

[4] id., Vol. I, Letter 17, p. 103.

gives free scope to his passions, but is reasoned into a state of calm content and unselfishness by his friend, Charles Maurice and finds happiness in the love of a poor orphan, Edith Alwynne.

The heroine, Gertrude Cathcart, "a woman of warm affections yielding herself to loose and declamatory principles, unfortunate from error and not from deliberate vice" is ruined by her unprincipled lover Edward D'Oyley, who, in calling all principles prejudices, obtains Gertrude's love and confidence. On finding out that he is a married man, Gertrude goes mad; she is a deplorable creature, "with her long, black hair dishevelled and loose on her shoulders, an infant clasped in her arms, her countenance ghastly, but suffused at this moment with a hectic flush" [1]. In an unprotected moment she takes poison, and leaves her baby to the care of others. Edmund Oliver and his wife superintend the education of the infant Gertrude, but the name of the mother is always avoided. Their sincerest wish is that the fate of the unhappy Gertrude may be "a warning to other females to go perseveringly onward in the straight path of unyielding purity and virtue" [2].

It is curious to consider that both Thomas Holcroft and Charles Lloyd think the anti-marriage principles dangerous for the unregulated female mind, not able to restrain the feelings by the power of Reason.

In another point Charles Lloyd is in advance of the novelists of his time as to him Nature is not only a source of admiration and love, but a healing power to man in his sorrow and desolation. "The wonderful effect which the general scene around him produced, won his mind irresistibly to a soft dawning of pleasure" [3].

[1] *Edmund Oliver,* Vol. II, Letter 56, p. 168.
[2] id., Vol. II.
[3] id., Vol. II, Letter 63, p. 208.

Recapitulating, we see that in spite of some relieving touches such as: a humorous outlook on life, and an attempt at characterization in the eccentric character of Miss Colerain [1], or the love of Mother Earth [2], and the beneficial influence of Nature [3], the novels of Thomas Holcroft, Robert Bage, Charlotte Smith, and Charles Lloyd all show the fatal tendency of giving us types instead of personalities. The hero does not appeal to our sympathy, because he is not human; he is nothing but a lay figure, propagating Revolutionary ideas.

The male characters are contrasted in the following traditional way: in each novel we find the hero, the natural man, led by reason, placed over against either the downright villain, or the weakling carried away by passion, but converted in thc end.

	Hero (simple honesty)	Villain (scheming hypocrisy)	Weakling [4]
I *Anna St. Ives*	Frank Henley		Coke Clifton
II *Man as he is*	Lyndsay		Sir George
III *The Banished Man*	The Chevalier	The Almoner	
IV *Edmund Oliver*	Charles Maurice	Edward d'Oyley	Edmund Oliver

In the female characters we see I Anna St. Ives, saved by the Natural Man, i.e. by reason; II Miss Colerain, true to her principles of Reason; III Miss Denzil, preferring a poor natural life to luxury; and IV Gertrude, destroyed by passion.

Taking for granted that the theme of the Revolutionary Novel is injustice and oppression, we find that in the novels

[1] v. R. Bage, *Man as he is.*
[2] Thomas Holcroft, *Anna St. Ives.*
[3] Charles Lloyd, *Edmund Oliver.*
[4] Cf. Dibelius II, *Englische Romankunst,* Kap. 2, p. 359.

we have discussed, the injustice is an individual case, the cause being adverse circumstances, scheming relations or inferior rank, whereas coming to Godwin's *Caleb Williams,* we see an instance of the helpless condition of the poorer classes in general; the institutions of society favouring the well-to-do classes who have made the laws, and refusing justice to the poor, or, as Caleb Williams expresses it himself in his memoirs: "Posterity seeing in my example what sort of evils are entailed upon mankind by society as it is at present constituted."

In every respect *Caleb Williams* is far superior to the above-mentioned novels and when we examine it closely. we come to the conclusion that the value of the book is to be found in the character of Falkland.

In this I differ from Saintsbury, who thinks: "One could sympathize with Falkland, but is not allowed to do so "because he is not human, except in his crime" [1], and also from Dibelius, who says:

"Bei Godwin bleiben Charakter und Taten Falklands ganz ohne inneren Zusammenhang; die psychologische Darstellung seines Verbrechers Falkland ist ihm nicht gelungen" [2].

It will be necessary to give a careful analysis of the character of Falkland as well as of the story of *Caleb Williams,* to prove my statement.

The story of Caleb Williams was the outcome of a fierce hatred of injustice and if any man was fit to write such a tale, it was William Godwin. The original title: *"Things as they are"* is rather suggestive; we immediately fill it up: "and as they ought not to be."

From his youth Godwin had a passion for justice; at Norwich, where he was sent in 1767, he had the free range

[1] Saintsbury, *The English novel,* Ch. IV, p. 168.

[2] Dibelius, *Englische Romankunst I,* Kap. 8, pp. 385-401.

of his tutor's library. "The books I read there", he says, "with the greatest transport were the early volumes of the English translation of the *Ancient History* of Rollin. Few bosoms ever beat with greater ardour than mine did, while perusing the story of the grand struggle of the Greeks for independence against the assaults of the Persian despot; and this scene awakened a passion in my soul, which will never cease but with life" [1].

All his convictions about justice, truth and liberty Godwin has laid down in his Political Justice, which he finished in Febr. 1793. In the same year he wrote the principal part of the novel *Caleb Williams,* of which he says himself: "It was the offspring of that temper of mind, in which the composition of my *Political Justice* left me."

When we come to the question, what Godwin's design was in writing this novel, the answer is not so easy to give.

In his autobiography he says: "In 1793 I commenced my *Caleb Williams,* with no further design than that of a slight composition, to produce a small supply of money, but never to be acknowledged: it improved and acquired weight in the manufacture" [2].

Other evidence we find in the Preface of 1794 and in that of 1832.

In the first Preface the author says that the book is meant for persons whom books of philosophy and science are never likely to reach; he wants to give a general review of the modes of domestic and unrecorded despotism, by which man becomes the destroyer of man, and in this way to teach a valuable lesson.

In the Preface of 1832 he says: "I bent myself to the conception of a series of adventures of flight and pursuit; the fugitive

[1] I quote from C. Kegan Paul, *W. Godwin;* Vol. I, Ch. I, p. 12.
[2] id., Vol. I, Ch. XIII, p. 361.

in perpetual apprehension of being overwhelmed with the worst calamities, and the pursuer, by his ingenuity and resources, keeping his victim in a state of the most fearful alarm."

Following this line of reasoning we come to nothing but the detective-novel that some people see in *Caleb Williams,* but though the two utterances seem to contradict each other, I think, we can safely accept the thought laid down in the first Preface: Godwin wanted to teach a valuable lesson. This statement is corroborated by what he says in the preface of 1832: "I will write a tale that shall constitute an epoch in the mind of the reader, that no one, after he has read it, shall ever be exactly the same man that he was before."

The thing in which his imagination revelled the most freely was, as he says himself: "the analysis of the private and internal operations of the mind, employing my metaphysical dissecting-knife in tracing and laying bare the involutions of motive, and recording the gradually accumulating impulses which led the personages I had to describe primarily to adopt the particular way of proceeding in which they afterwards embarked."

It seems curious that the philosophic Godwin, whose theories are all based on Reason, creates about his hero Falkland an atmosphere of romance, an air of mystery, such as we find about Edmund Twyford in the *Old English Baron* by Clara Reeve, where the key gives way to his hand only, and every door in the house flies open, the moment Edmund enters the hall of his ancestors, or such as we find about the awe-inspiring Montoni in his Gothic castle of Udolpho [1]; it seems curious, but then William Godwin was more than the calm, merely intellectual reasoner that he seemed to be.

When we consider how he was the confessor as it were, of young men who brought to him their difficulties, intellectual

[1] *The Mysteries of Udolpho* by Mrs. Radcliffe.

and social, and who confided to him their sorrows and sins [1], we can see him like those in his own time, who could get beyond his shell, as the eager, sympathetic man who had not forgotten the days of his own youth, who knew that "there is more between heaven and earth than is dreamt of in your philosophy." As such he revealed himself, when he wrote to H. B. Rosser, a student at Cambridge, March 7, 1820: "All that I see, the earth, the sea, the rivers, the trees, the clouds, animals, and, most of all, man, fills me with love and astonishment. My soul is full to bursting with the mystery of all this and I love it the better for its mysteriousness. It is too wonderful for me; it is past finding out, but it is beyond expression delicious."

In his fifteenth and sixteenth year (1772—1773) Godwin read the whole of Shakespeare and even planned an epic of Brute; in his letters we see how his style was influenced by the speech of Brutus in the Forum, when he writes: "Had you rather have nominal possession of power with your hands free for the purposes of corruption, but chained up from the exertion of every virtuous effort, than have the real possession of power able to make every act of your administration a blessing to Britain, to Europe and mankind"; and just as Shakespeare makes it clear to us, how Brutus, the noblest of them all, could kill Julius Caesar, so Godwin shows us, how it was possible that Falkland, a man of inflexible integrity could commit a secret murder and persecute an innocent man.

This innocent man is Caleb Williams, the secretary, who driven by an insatiate curiosity, cannot help studying his master's character and prying into his secrets, and who, after having found out the fatal truth that Mr. Falkland is the

[1] cf. Kegan Paul Vol. II, Ch. I p. 106.
[2] cf. id., Vol. I, Ch. III p. 76.

murderer, finds the tables turned upon him, when the victim, instead of remaining at his servant's mercy, becomes the tyrant ant pursuer.

The story is as carefully built up as the plot of a drama; the episodes [1] are not only connected in spirit, they also help in furthering the story. All of them tell a tale, either of chivalry or of injustice.

As a young man, at the age at which the grand tour is usually made, Falkland, the hero, of the story stays in Italy for a long time; he is well read in the Italian poets and keenly alive to the sentiments of birth, honour, and chivalry.

He is a great favourite with the Italian noblemen, as well as with the fair sex and is soon engaged in an affair of honour. In the opinion of the Italians, the life of a man is of very little consideration when honour is concerned and an indignity cannot be expiated but with blood.

Here the idea of murder is mentioned for the first time, showing how Falkland's mind imbibes that thought in the time of its growth. Influenced as he was by Rousseau, Godwin set a great value on the power of education and surroundings.

In this affair of honour Falkland's reason conquers his passion, and he abstains from a duel with Count Malvesi, though he makes it clear to him that his temper is not less impetuous and fiery than that of his opponent and that a peaceful solution would have been impossible, if the challenge had been public; then dishonour could only have been expiated by blood.

[1] Cf. William Godwin. *Caleb Williams,* Half Forgotten books.
Episodes:

p. 13, Lady Lucretia Pisani.
p. 50, Emily Melville.
p. 90, Hawkins.
p. 172, A peasant accused of murder.
p. 247, Brightwel in prison.
p. 297, the robbers.
p. 372, Mrs. Marney.
p. 375, Mr. Spurrel.
p. 404, Laura Denison.
p. 427, Mr. Collins.

The idea of a murder is no longer outside Falkland's range of thought; we shall see that every following occurrence brings the possibility nearer and nearer. Falkland returns to England and finds in his neighbourhood the man who is to become his greatest enemy in the person of Mr. Tyrrel a brutal English squire, a coarse bully with enormous physical strength, and without any refinement. At first he tries to convince Mr. Tyrrel of the purity of his intentions and settles the first quarrel by saying that precaution in this stage can be dishonourable to neither, but the time may come that the strife leads to consequences that he shudders to think of. His reason and philosophy induce him to suppress his rage. He thinks that: "In the society of men we must have something to endure, as well as to enjoy. No man must think that the world was made for him. Let us take things as we find them; and accommodate ourselves as we can to unavoidable circumstances." After Falkland's departure, Mr. Tyrrel wonders what possessed him, that he did not kick his enemy! "But that is all to come!"

Falkland's friend, Mr. Clare, sees the danger that is threatening and when he feels his end is near, admonishes Falkland to beware of Mr. Tyrrel and of his own impetuosity, and points out the urgent necessity of justice and reason. He has a painful presentiment that Falkland's history might be changed into misery and guilt.

After Mr. Clare's death Tyrrel's hatred strengthens more and more: his cousin Emily's praises of Falkland fan the flame of his envy; the assistance Falkland gives to Hawkins, a tenant of Mr. Tyrrel, who had provoked his master's rage by his independent mind, the way, in which Falkland saves Emily from the infamy that Mr. Tyrrel had planned for her, the fact that Mr. Tyrrel at the rural assembly overawes every one but Falkland, all these circumstances hasten the catastrophe.

Spurned by Mr. Falkland, hunted out of society, Mr. Tyrrel with one blow of his muscular arm levels his enemy with the earth; the latter has scarcely risen, when Mr. Tyrrel repeats his blow; Falkland is again brought to the earth. In this situation Mr. Tyrrel kicks his prostrate enemy. — To Falkland disgrace in public is worse than death; to make matters worse, he is baffled of his vengeance, as Mr. Tyrrel is found dead in the street by some of the company, having been murdered at the distance of a few yards from the assembly-house.

There is a whisper that Falkland may be guilty, and indeed the catastrophe is the beginning of a gloomy and unsociable melancholy in Falkland's life; he, who was an object of envy, now becomes an object of compassion. Life is no longer a joy to him, but a heavy burden; still he disdains to fly from calumny and manages to clear his reputation. After some time the murderer is found in the person of Hawkins, who confesses his guilt, but there are persons by whom this is denied.

Mr. Falkland is getting excessively sensitive in matters of honour and suspects some latent insinuation on every possible occasion; he indulges in lonely rambles in the country; as a Justice of the Peace he cannot condemn a peasant accused of murder. After he has heard his secretary exclaim in the garden: "Mr. Falkland is the murderer," he disappears and is supposed to have gone on one of his accustomed rambles.

Now that he is in the power of his secretary, life becomes unbearable to him and he resolves to save his reputation, whatever may be the sufferings to another.

This resolution leads up to the turning-point in the story, the scene, in which Falkland confesses his guilt, but at the same time condemns Caleb Williams to a life of fear and persecution in saying: "You have sold yourself; you shall continue in my service, but can never share my affection. If ever an unguarded word escape from your lips, if ever you excite my jealousy or suspicion, expect to pay for it by your death or worse" [1].

And the fate that awaits Caleb Williams, is certainly worse than death. For him no quiet, no joy, no friends; barred out from all communication with his fellow-creatures, driven from every place, where he hopes to find peace at last. As soon as he has won Mr. Forster's friendship, he is accused of theft and sent to prison; he feels the power of the rich, who have made the laws; it embitters him and he refuses to sign a paper, declaring Falkland to be innocent. He is followed by a spy in the pay of Falkland, he is detested by every one, forbidden to leave England and seek a new home.

At last he resolves openly to accuse Mr. Falkland; he applies to the chief magistrate of the metropolitan town of the county, in which Mr. Falkland resides. The latter is summoned and is brought in a chair, looking haggard and ghost-like.

Caleb Williams is deeply touched by this sight and wishes he could recall the last four days, to make it undone, but it is too late.

He repents that he has had recourse to the law, because, on seeing his master, he is once more convinced that Mr. Falkland's nature is so noble that he could not have resisted a frank and fervid expostulation, if Caleb had tried again.

At first Mr. Falkland is filled with indignation, but understanding Caleb's feelings of compunction and grief, he throws himself into his servant's arms with the words: "Williams, you have conquered. I see too late the greatness and elevation of your mind."

[1] *Caleb Williams,* Vol. I, Ch. VI, p. 187.

Falkland survives this dreadful event but three days, and Caleb constantly has his master's image before him; full of forgiveness he realizes that a nobler spirit lived not among the sons of men.

"But of what use are talents and sentiments in the corrupt wilderness of human society? It is rank and rotten soil, from which every finer shrub draws poison as it grows" [1].

Though Falkland was not a paragon of virtue, he was certainly one of the finer shrubs of the earth and the poison that he drew from the rank and rotten soil, was "the poison of chivalry." It was Godwins belief that the characters of men originate in their external circumstances [1], and that is why he shows us Ferdinand Falkland as a young man with frank and ingenuous manners, an open character and a warm enthusiasm for what is true and noble; resolute and brave in difficulties, with an impetuous temper, it is true, but able to subdue it by reason. He considered it a privilege to belong to the aristocracy, and it was his ambition to be looked upon as a perfect gentleman.

This is just where his weakness comes in. Brailsford has said that Falkland personifies the spirit of chivalry at its best and at its worst [2], and indeed, the worst part of his ambition is that he is not satisfied with being a perfect gentleman, but that he wants to be looked upon as a perfect gentleman. It is the inordinate love of reputation that becomes his ruling passion. When he abstains from a duel in Italy, it is, because he knows that the reputation of his courage is sufficiently established; this conviction co-operating with his reason enables him to control his temper.

In his relations to his neighbours he is a man with gentle and refined manners, never showing off as the superior, and still

[1] *Caleb Williams*, Postscript, p. 449.

[2] H. N. Brailsford, *Shelley, Godwin and their Circle*, Ch. IV, p. 144.

behaving with such dignity that he is felt to be so all the same; a man with a delicate consideration for others, but who makes them feel that he never gives way, if once he has got a claim to a thing.

Mr. Clare, his best friend, sees, how, when once he has put his mind on a certain object, he persists with obstinacy, till at length he has carried his point; this consideration makes Mr. Clare fear that Falkland's strong will may undo him, when it comes into contact with his sensitive point, an imagined attack on his honour.

Though a kind man, he impresses people by his authority and his presence of mind, and no formality or reserve are wanted to inspire respect.

He is a man of strong emotions, sympathizing with people, whose independence is attacked (Hawkins) and burning with indignation, when tyranny reigns free. (Emily).

After the fatal death of Mr. Tyrrel there is a complete change in him which people ascribe to the fact that the insult cannot be made up for, and to the accusation of murder. He has become a melancholy man, reserved and incommunicative, proud and independent; he avoids other people as much as he can; it seems as if he keeps them at a distance and even does not grant himself the comfort of communicating his griefs to a confidential friend from the motive that he does not want to be a burden to any one. In this as in all other respects he shows great consideration for others, and in the eyes of his domestics he is a benevolent master; but at times his reason cannot control his temper, and at such moments he is peevish and even tyrannical. His servants know him as a man who is a stranger to pleasure, who is never seen to smile; but in spite of his solitary, singular habits, he is to them a being of a superior order. The strangest point in his behaviour is, that, though after an outburst of rage he is doubly attentive to the person on whom he has vented his wrath [1], he never accounts for his fury and for that reason some people consider him as disordered in his intellect at times.

He is acutely sensitive and often flies from the intercourse with human beings, a pale, haggard, solitary man. He knows his own weakness, but he cannot overcome it and is too proud to confide in others; after his confession to Caleb he says: "I am as much the fool of fame as ever; I will leave behind me a spotless and illustrious name; I want no pity, I desire no consolation, I will at least preserve my fortitude to the last" [2].

It is not personal hatred that makes him pursue Caleb Williams; wherever he can, he sends him secret assistance, but the thing he has set his mind upon is to preserve his reputation, which he loves more than the whole world, at all costs, and he will not rest, till he has carried his point. His greatest punishment he finds in the destruction of that for the sake of which alone he consented to exist.

In Falkland Godwin has given the character of a man, neither ideal, nor ordinary; a man who, in spite of his noble aspirations, could not be "master of his fate", because of his one great weakness; it is not so much fate that is against him, as his prevailing passion for honour.

The great difference between *Caleb Williams* and the novels discussed above is, that the preaching is not given in sermonizing chapters by way of interludes, but the principles are interwoven with the story as well as with the character, so that it is difficult to separate one from the other. In *Caleb Williams,* Godwin has once more stated his opinion that the principles which are to lead to a healthier state of society are justice, truth, and reason.

[1] *Caleb Williams,* Vol. I, Ch. I, p. 8.
id., Vol. II, Ch. VI, p. 186.

Introduction to Chapter II

The Ideas of the Second Period: The Sociological Novel, influenced by the Industrial Revolution

The words: 'Industrial Revolution' call up before our minds a series of great problems [1].

The question of unemploymcnt has become an urgent one; the gulf between capital and labour widens; great strikes reveal the growth of discontent.

The remedies proposed are of various kinds; wc have only to mention Chartism, Christian Socialism, the Oxford Movement, the Young England party and the Trade-Unions to give an idea of the manner in which mind and soul were brought into play, to find a way out of the bewildering perplexity of problems. Society showed a new aspect; industrial England, the England of manufacturers and tradespeople had replaced the England of squires. The political change brought about by the Reform Act (1832) was no more considered all sufficient; the cry was no longer the Rights of Man, as in the time of the Revolutionists, but the Rights of the worker and the necessity of a living wage; injustice and inequality are felt even more intensely than in the preceding period, but the remedy is no longer sought in a reliance on Reason; on the conntrary a reaction has set in, proclaiming the

[1] Cf. L. Cazamian, *Le Roman Social en Angleterre*, Ch. I.
Dr. H. Jansonius, *Some Aspects of Business Life*, Ch. III.
Dr. J. J. v. Dullemen, *Mrs. Gaskell, Novelist and Biographer*, Ch. .

ascendancy of the heart over the head; the preaching of Rousseau is replaced by that of Carlyle.

The great novelists of this time, Charles Dickens, Charles Kingsley, Mrs. Gaskell, and George Eliot are all influenced more or less by Carlyle and in their sociological novels they have popularized the thoughts of their great master. It will serve our purpose to state the principal of those ideas:

First there is a fight against the spirit of industrialism, as Cazamian says: "Chacun pour soi et la loi anglaise pour tous, telle est la morale de l'industrialisme"[1]; then there is a fight against materialism, against competition, against the wrong conceptions of liberty and equality; there is above all a fight against preoccupation with self.

Carlyle sees a remedy for the evils of his time in work, well-chosen and done faithfully and with love; in noble loyalty in return for noble guidance, in combined human endeavours, not to see what lies dimly at a distance, but to do what lies clearly at hand, in resolutely struggling forward, but above all in the regeneration of the individual and in mutual helpfulness.

Carlyle has an open eye for the needs of the workers and the problems of his time, when he says:

"This largest of questions, this question of Work and Wages, which ought, had we heeded Heaven's voice, to have begun two generations ago or more, cannot be delayed longer without hearing Earth's voice. — Man will actually need to have his debts and earnings a little better paid by man; which, let Parliaments speak of them or be silent of them, are eternally his due from man, and cannot, without penalty and at length not without death-penalty be withheld[2]; and again:

[1] L. Cazamian, *Le Roman Social en Angleterre,* Ch. I, p. 27.

[2] Carlyle, *Past and Present* Book III, Ch. XIII.

"Injustice, infidelity to truth and fact and Nature's order, being properly the one evil under the sun, and the feeling of injustice the one intolerable pain under the sun, our grand question as to the condition of these working men would be: Is it just?" [1]

But at the same time he gives an earnest warning that something more is required than obtaining a living wage. In *Past and Present* [2] he says: "The wages of every noble Work do yet lie in Heaven or else Nowhere. Was it thy aim and life-purpose to be filled with good things for thy heroism; to have a life of pomp and ease, and be what men call "happy" in this world, or in any other world? I answer for thee deliberately, No. The whole spiritual secret of the new epoch lies in this, that thou canst answer for thyself, with thy whole clearness of head and heart, deliberately, No!"

The best reward for work done, a man has who can say with Shakespeare's Portia: "He is well paid, who is well satisfied."

The best happiness, Carlyle says, a man has, who is aware that liberty means finding out the right path and walking thereon, to learn, or to be taught what work he actually is able to do.

"Sure enough, of all paths a man could strike into, there is, at any given moment, a best path for every man; a thing which, here and now, it were of all things wisest for him to do. It is not a question of fighting, it is a question of working.

The epic verily is not: Arms and the Man, but: Tools and the Man."

Carlyle is convinced that man will mislead himself in seeking equality; in his opinion equality of men is a thing unnatural and unobtainable.

[1] Carlyle, *Chartism,* p. 25.

[2] Carlyle, *Past and Present,* Book III, Ch. XII.

"True enough, man is forever the born thrall of certain men, born master of certain other men, born equal of certain others, let him acknowledge the fact or not."

He comes to the conclusion that what work, the grandest of human interests, requires is organizing.

"The task will be hard, but no noble task was ever easy. Put forth thy hand, in God's name; know that "impossible", where Truth and Mercy and the everlastlng Voice of Nature order, has no place in the brave man's dictionary. Ask no man's counsel, but thy own only and God's."

But the only way to see the right path, to understand the nobleness of work is a 'Return to Nature'.

What Carlyle means by a 'Return to Nature' is quite a different thing from the 'Return to Nature' of the writers in the Revolutionary period. To Carlyle it means a resurrection of soul and conscience, a regeneration of the inner man.

"O brother, we must if possible resuscitate some soul and conscience in us, exchange our dilettantisms for sincerities, our dead hearts of stone for living hearts of flesh" [1].

The same thought is repeated again and again by Charles Dickens, Mrs. Gaskell, Charles Kingsley and George Eliot; man's true good lies within him, not without, and the only way to banish injustice, the only solid reformation, as Carlyle says at the end of *Signs of the Times* [2] is, what each begins and perfects on himself.

Carlyle had a great faith in the imperishable dignity of man and his high vocation and believed that the very unrest of mankind and its discontent contained matter of promise.

We find the same tone of hopefulness in the sociological novel of this period. The evils of the time are laid bare without shrinking, but however dark the night may be

[1] Carlyle, *Past and Present,* Book I, Ch. IV.

[2] Edinburgh Review, Vol. 49. (1829).

dawn is near! The watchwords, used by the novelists are no longer Truth and Liberty, but: A better Understanding between master and man, Regeneration and Organization.

These watchwords represent the leading thoughts in the sociological novel of the second period:

Dissatisfaction with the existing conditions in the exhortation: "Put your hand to the plough to bring about a better understanding."

Return to Nature, in the reformation of self as the first step to reform the world.

Simplification as regards social life in the attempt to remove the glaring contrasts between rich and poor by organization and co-operation.

CHAPTER II

The Sociological Novel. influenced by the Industrial Revolution

Charles Dickens, Mrs. Gaskell, Charles Kingsley, George Eliot.

In considering the psychological element in the sociological novels written by Dickens, I have chosen *Hard Times* as a subject for discussion, because it is the only novel, in which he gives a picture of the workman at war with capital. It is true, we find a good example of this question in *The Chimes,* but we hardly look upon this story as a novel; moreover, Cazamian has given us such an exact analysis of this story as to make it superfluous to treat it again.

It is interesting to see, how much some of the opinions about *Hard Times* clash [1].

Macaulay is disgusted with the book for the hopeless misconceptions of the problems and methods of Political Economy; George Gissing says: "It seems to me that Dickens has produced a book, quite unworthy of him, and this wholly apart from the question of its economic teaching" [2], whereas Ruskin, though fully aware of the defects of the book, writes in the first Essay of *Unto this Last.* "To my mind, in several respects, it is the greatest he has written."

Gissing calls it a book that is practically forgotten, and there is a truth in that, but I disagree with him, when he says that there is little in it that demands attention. It is exactly in this novel that Dickens makes quite clear to us,

[1] Dr. H. Jansonius, *Some Aspects of Business Life,* p. 51.

[2] G. Gissing, *Charles Dickens,* Ch. II, p. 24.

what he has found as the best remedy for the social evils of his time, and in this he shows himself the true follower of Carlyle, to whom he inscribed the book. Of Carlyle's words: "It is the heart always that sees, before the head can see," Dickens gives us an illustration in the character of Louisa Gradgrind, and if it were only for this character, *Hard Times* should not be a forgotten book.

Louisa is the daughter of Mr. Gradgrind, the great factory-owner of Coketown, a man of realities, a man of facts and calculations, who has brought up his children, Louisa and Tom upon the belief that all things that cannot be reasoned out, are sentimental humbug.

We can see little Loo, at twelve years old, watching the bright sparks as they drop upon the hearth, with a dreamy expression in her eyes; she, whose imagination has been starved, who has never been roaming about in the fairyland of childhood and still with something in her, saying: "I wonder."

We can see her silenced, but not satisfied, when her father overwhelms her with the words: "Louisa, never wonder, by means of addition, subtraction, multiplication and division settle everything somehow, and never wonder" [1].

To the superficial eye the quiet girl gives in and learns what her father wants her to learn, acts as he wants her to act, but deep down in her heart there is a craving for beauty, a hunger for love, that nobody knows of, except her brother Tom, who profits by it for his own selfish purposes.

When a girl of fifteen or sixteen, she is discovered by her father, while she is standing on tiptoe, trying to peep in at the hidden glories of the circus; her only explanation, on being rebuked for vulgar curiosity, is: "I am tired of everything."

There is a great difference between her and Tom; her

[1] Ch. Dickens, *Hard Times,* Ch. VIII.

brother promises himself that in the future he will recompense himself for the way in which he has been brought up, whereas Loo who has nothing rebellious in her, is depressed by all that is wanting in her life and in herself. Tom says that he does not miss anything in her, but she answers: "I do know better, Tom, and am very sorry for it."

Thinking her own thoughts in her own quiet, honest way, she sees that she cannot make her brother like life at home, that there is something dried up in her, something that she cannot define, but which she knows to be of the utmost value. She has not the energy to free herself, she sees the future before her, not as a land of promise, but as a waste land of monotony and she consents to marry Mr. Bounderby, her father's friend, with a cold indifference that is too much even for her matter-of-fact father. The only thing that she insists on, is that her answer shall be an honest one, and indeed, it is not love that is asked for, as her father says: "Mr. Bounderby does not do you the injustice, or does not do himself the injustice of pretending to anything fanciful, fantastic or (I am using synonymous terms) sentimental." During the conversation with her father Louisa is calm and self-controlled; only for one moment it seems as if the fire, which is smouldering in her, is going to flame up. It seems as if she is to tell her father about that voice deep down in her heart; it is only one wavering moment; it passes, and the only comfort for her is in the contemplation: "Life is short, it does not matter."

But in spite of everything there is in her a whisper: "It does matter," a still voice that cannot be silenced, however much she tries.

She is convinced that she cannot confide in her father, who quite misunderstands her bitter words: "What do I know of tastes and fancies, of aspirations and affections, of all that part of my nature in which such light things might have been nourished? You have been so careful of me, that I never had a child's heart. You have trained me so well, that I never dreamed a child's dream. You have dealt so wisely with me, father, from my cradle to this hour, that I never had a child's belief or a child's fear."

She lets the moment go by and shuts herself up in a proud reserve; she cannot bear to be pitied and keeps her little friend Sissy at a distance, after she has seen the look of wonder in her eyes, when the intended marriage is spoken of.

The only moment when she is a little shaken in her reserved composure, is, when Tom calls her a first-rate sister, little realizing, that it is the rich brother-in-law that Tom sees in Mr. Bounderby. Now and afterwards all her thoughts are for her brother; it is the only consolation in her married life that she can assist him, but this feeling cannot fill the emptiness of her life.

To Mr. Harthouse, the young cynic, she appears as a reserved, cold and proud woman, who soon betrays herself before his watchful eyes as sensitively ashamed of her husband's bragging humility and touchingly pleased at the slightest attention on her brother's part.

He knows how to find a place in the life of this woman, to all appearances so perfectly self-reliant, but in reality so badly in want of human sympathy.

As to her, his cynic view of life is in a way a revelation to her, for, if it is true that feeling and imagination are nothing but humbug, then she has not missed anything in life.

At this crisis, life brings her into contact with two of the working-people, Stephen Blackpool and Rachel. Stephen, who is not at all a type of perfection, as Gissing wants to make us believe, but only a simple, honest man who asks the right to do his work and get his due of happiness, as well as the rich people; who sees the greatest injustice, not in an unequal share of wealth, but in the haughty way, in which the life of working-people is spoken of, the way in which the employers treat their hands as figures or machines, without any fellow-feeling; a man who rebels against the misery of his married life, from which there is no escape, because he is poor, who nearly succumbs to the temptation of suffering his wife to put an end to her life without interfering and who is only checked by the rescuing influence of Rachel.

It is for the first time that Louisa comes face to face with anything like individuality in connection with the factory-hands. Up to that moment they had been to her nothing but the grumbling, discontented crowd; it is for the first time that she comes into close touch with the tender feelings that live in their hearts and it is a revelation that shines like a flash-light into her soul, when she sits there in Stephen's little room, "young, and handsome, with dark thinking eyes and a still way."

From that time there is an unceasing struggle in her mind; she wants to believe in a wider and nobler humanity, but again and again she is attacked by doubts, and these doubts are strengthened in her intercourse with Mr. Harthouse. She does not love him, but he has a stifling effect on her and it is a relief to her to hear in all his utterances that all she fears she has missed in life, is hollow and worthless.

Gradually he establishes a confidence with her, from which her husband is excluded, a confidence into which her love for Tom has betrayed her.

There is nothing in the remembrances of her home and childhood to sustain her, and yet, when she sees her little sister with her arm round Sissy's neck, she knows that feeling and fancy are not hollow and worthless and again the still voice in her whispers: "It does matter". And it is this which saves her both from indifference and from disgrace.

Now the moment has come that she confesses to her father that she has grown up, battling every inch of her way, to find out at last that his philosophy and his teaching will not save her, and to know that it is her little sister's greatest blessing that she has avoided her way. She opens her heart freely to her father, who, touched by his child's utter misery, for the first time in his life is shaken in his reliance on the mighty power of fact, and hesitatingly speaks his doubt: "Some persons hold that there is a wisdom of the Head, and that there is a wisdom of the Heart. I have not supposed so; but, as I have said, I mistrust myself now. I have supposed the Head to be all-sufficient. It may not be all-sufficient."

Louisa has run away from her husband and escaped from Mr. Harthouse's mesmeric influence, and though she has told all to her father, her pride makes her hide her distress from others, but Sissy with fine feeling knows how so soothe her, and to make her stick to the newly-found truth that the imaginative qualities, so sadly neglected in her youth, are the things that make life worth living.

Disappointed in Tom, she still does all that is in her power, to save his reputation, but it is in vain, and her father fulfils the urgent request of Stephen, who has been accused of theft, openly to declare that his son Tom is the culprit.

Stephen meets with an accident and is found at the bottom of Old Hell Shaft. Up to the last moment it is "all a muddle" to him, and his greatest grievance that the poor are mistrusted and suspected; his dying prayer is for a better understanding on both sides.

Louisa, watching the fire as before, now sees the future, not as a heavenly vista of personal happiness, but as a life of duty, with her work clearly cut out for her, "trying hard to know her humbler fellow-creatures, and to beautify their lives of machinery and reality with those imaginative graces and delights, without which the heart of infancy will wither up, the sturdiest physical manhood will be morally stark death, and the plainest national prosperity figures can show, will be the Writing on the Wall" [1].

In Louisa's father we see the converted man; just as Falkland in Godwin's *Caleb Williams* at last has found that all must give way to Truth and Reason, so Mr. Gradgrind's eyes have been opened to the truth that the Heart is of greater value than the Head, that benevolence and fellow-feeling and a better understanding between high and low are necessary for the happiness of all. Aged and bent and quite bowed down; and yet he looked a wiser and a better man than in the days when in his life he wanted nothing but Facts.

Im emphasizing the urgent necessity of improvement, Dickens was not a fighter in the real sense of the word; the social question to him was merely a moral question; the remedy he saw in a better education of the people.

The words in *A Christmas Carol* spoken by the Spirit of the Past: "This boy is Ignorance. This girl is Want. Beware them both, and all of their degree, but most of all beware this boy, for on his brow, I see that written which is Doom, unless the writing be erased," were at the bottom of Dickens's philosophy. In his heart of hearts he was convinced that the writing would be erased and that a better education would lead to a state of Peace upon Earth and Good-will unto all men.

Though Dickens was not a Socialist in name, he still based his philosophy on the same ideas that we find in various social systems; though different in means and ways they are at one in the thought that the true end of human existence

[1] Charles Dickens, *Hard Times,* Book III, Ch. IX, p. 398.

is that the soul should be possessed and exercised by the Love-Spirit and by the principle of active, unselfish self-denial [1], in the ideal of converting all labour from a toil into a pleasure [2], and in the conviction that far more happiness can be attained by union than by disunion [3].

"Good - will unto all men," also forms the basis of Mrs Gaskell's teaching in her two sociological novels, *Mary Barton* and *North and South.* Both of them treat the relation between employer and workman; *Mary Barton* as seen from the worker's standpoint, *North and South* as seen from the master's point of view, but there is an idea, underlying the facts in both books that binds them together: the thought that workman as well as employer have been wanting in the attempt to understand each other better and thus to bridge over the great gulf between them. — With an intimate knowledge of the evils of life in the factory-towns, she takes us there, that we may see with our own eyes how the workers live, but, above all, that we may understand what they think and feel, for just as to Dickens, the social question is to Mrs. Gaskell a moral question.

She too sees the remedy in an awakening of the soul, a regeneration of the inner being, and as a necessary result, a better understanding between rich and poor.

In both novels we have the story of a conversion; in *Mary Barton* we meet Mr. Carson, the hard, unfeeling master, broken down by the loss of his only son, swearing revenge on the workman who has murdered him.

Mrs. Gaskell wrote this book a short time after she had lost her only son, and her own suffering enabled her to see how a great sorrow can bring about a thoroughly different

[1] James Pierrepont Greaves.

[2] Charles Fourier.

[3] Robert Owen.

outlook on life. Still there is something unnatural in the suddenness of the change in the character of Mr. Carson.

By chance Mr. Carson hears John Barton, the disillusioned and embittered workman, who has murdered young Carson, in order to intimidate the class of tyrants, confess his guilt; his first impulse is, to hand him over to the police, feeling this act as a revenge that he owes to his son, but, walking, home, he notices the occurrences of daily life with a strange intensity, such as we often realize in times of great sorrow, and the words of a little girl who has been badly treated by a big boy in the street: "He did not know, what he was doing," haunt him so much that, in coming home, he opens the family bible; his eye falls upon the fly-leaf where the name of the son was written together with the day of his birth, but then he turns up the page where he can find the words that haunt him and he reads the account of Jesus' sufferings and forgiving love and all night long the struggle in him goes on, but in the end the Spirit of Love gains the victory and Mr. Carson again goes to his enemy's house, only to find him dying.

John Barton dies in Mr. Carson's arms, the proud employer now humbled and forgiving, praying aloud: "Forgive us our trespasses, as we forgive them that trespass against us."

All things that have mattered most to Mr. Carson in life up to now, are as nothing compared with the loss of his son. What is it to be rich, to be a man of standing among the merchant-princes? There is only one wish in him now, "that none might suffer from the cause, from which he had suffered; that a perfect understanding, and complete confidence and love might exist between masters and men; that the truth might be recognized that the interests of one were the interests of all, and as such, required the consideration and deliberation of all; that hence it was most desirable to have educated workers, capable of judging, not mere machines of ignorant men" [1].

To his dying-day Mr. Carson is considered hard and cold by those who casually see him, or superficially know him, but taught by suffering and the Spirit of Christ, his stern, energetic mind influences others and his regeneration is the origin of many improvements in the system of employment in the factory-town, where he lives.

In *North and South* we find the character of the employer better analysed; the story was written seven years later; Mrs. Gaskell's mind had grown calmer and experience had taught her to look at the social question, not only as the problem of the injustice suffered by the hands, but also as the problem of the responsibility on the employers' side.

In September 1854 the first instalment of *North and South* was published in *Household Words*, under the editorship of Charles Dickens, the same magazine, in which *Hard Times* had appeared in April—August 1854.

Mrs. Gaskell had a great advantage over Dickens, living as she was at Manchester, and in the sphere of her husband, the Rev. William Gaskell. In comparing *Hard Times* with Mrs. Gaskell's novels, we cannot help noticing how much more lifelike her characters are, and how much better she knew the working-people than Dickens.

In *North and South* Mrs. Gaskell describes Mr. Thornton, the self-made man, who does not look upon life as a time for enjoyment, but as a time for action and exertion, who is very hard upon the workers who claim their rights, before they have realized their duties; he is disappointed in his love for Margaret Hale, the beautiful, proud, refined girl, who sees in Mr. Thornton nothing but the money-making tradesman of the North, whose mind is closed to the softer influences

[1] cf. Mrs. Gaskell, *Mary Barton,* XXXVII.

of the South. Mr. Thornton mistrusts his workmen and their intentions, especially one Higgins, who is dismissed from the mills as a rebel. At the advice of Margaret, Higgins goes to Mr. Thornton with the request to take him back; he wants to make up for the past and to assist the children of Boucher, a victim of the lock-out who has drowned himself in his despair.

Thornton suspects Higgins's motives and sends him away, but is all the same struck by the fact that Higgins has been waiting five hours to be admitted into his presence.

Thornton hesitatingly asks himself the question, if his willingness to grant Higgins's request may be influenced by the circumstance that Margaret has advised him to go, but then it is always his greatest desire that men shall recognize his justice and so he speaks to Higgins again. This leads to a sort of friendship between the two men, who, before, have called each other, an impudent liar and a mischief-maker on one side, and a bull-dog and a hard, cruel master on the other side. Now that Mr. Thornton pretty often comes to Higgins's house, the latter's opinion changes; he says that Mr. Thornton is really two chaps, and that he knows the chap now that is a man, not a master.

Thornton has been impressed by the miserable meal that is dished up for Higgins and the children and it sets him thinking.

The result is that he puts into practice the idea which he first thought impracticable, to build a dining-room and kitchen for the workmen, on such a plan that he does not interfere with their independence. He is very pleased when they ask him to come in and take a snack, because it enables him to know some of his men, when they talk freely before him.

Gradually this pleasure becomes one of the greatest interests in his life; he is no longer centred on himself as an employer, but begins to look with their eyes.

And then the crisis in business comes: the strike and as

a consequence the work done badly by unskilled hands, the new machinery useless for want of orders, no capital laid by and before him loss of position; it is a great blow to his pride, because "he was but like many others — men, women, and children — alive to distant, and dead to near things. He sought to possess the influence of a name in foreign countries and far-away seas — to become the head of a firm that should be known for generations; and it had taken him long silent years to come even to a glimmering of what he might be now, to-day, here in his own town, his own factory, among his own people"[1] but it is this glimmering of what he may be to others that saves him from entering into a risky speculation which might be the ruin of many.

He does not succumb to the temptation of saving his reputation as a wealthy merchant, because he feels it would be at the risk of losing his peace of mind.

He will sooner consent to be only a manager and thus keep in touch with the workmen than be the partner of a money-making man without a sense of responsibility.

The change in his inner being is felt by some of his men, who understand his difficulties and are drawn to him; they take no offence at his abrupt commands, when he is pressed down by worries.

He does not lose heart and though he may make great blunders, he will try to be brave in setting to afresh. He knows that, reserved as he is, he will never be popular, but with all these drawbacks he feels that he is on the right path, and that, starting from a kind of friendship with one, he is becoming acquainted with many and that they are teaching each other; so with an unshrinking honesty he goes on and he appears before Margaret who has inherited a large fortune from her father's friend and is now his land-

[1] Mrs. Gaskell, *North and South*, Ch. L.

lord, as a changed man, looking older and careworn, but with a noble composure and dignity; he is not afraid to acknowledge his want of success, because he has won the sympathy of his workmen and is convinced that, though conflicts will come, they need not be the bitter, venomous sources of hatred they have hitherto been. And it is his glory that strong in his own happiness of calling Margaret his own, he will be able to continue his experiments.

Mrs. Gaskell, just like Dickens, sees the dawning light in the union of employer and workman, in the endeavour to obtain a better understanding between master and men, more than in a union of the workmen among themselves and it is in this respect that they differ from Charles Kingsley, the strong, energetic Rector of Eversley. "Peace upon Earth" was not in the first place his ideal.

W. R. Greg [1] has called Kingsley and Carlyle the most combative writers of their age.

Kingsley scattered his problems among the people, to wake them up and make them think, whether they liked it or not. He was greatly influenced by Carlyle, but the living force in his life was Frederick Denison Maurice, as he has said himself: "I owe all that I am to Maurice, I live to interpret him to the people of England."

"Maurice is the most beautiful human soul whom God has ever allowed me to meet with upon this earth" [2], whereas on the other hand Maurice himself felt stirred by the admiring love of Kingsley, as we see from the letter to the Rev. Charles Kingsley 1849:

"I felt that sympathy and love can bring music out of any instrument; mine is often sadly jarred and out of tune

[1] Cf. W. R. Greg, *Literary and Social Judgments.*

[2] *The Life of Frederick Denison Maurice.* Chiefly told in his own letters, edited by his son, p. 554.

and gives forth nothing but harsh notes. But when you played upon it, I found that good could come out of it" [1].

It was indeed a wonderful interplay of inspiration, for as J. M. Ludlow has said: "One remarkable characteristic of Mr. Maurice was this: he always went below a man's words to his real meaning, in many cases thus explaining the man to himself" [2].

Kingsley with his unflinching courage, inspires others, not to fear, to attack the evils of the time, to look the storm straight in the face, to do the work that cannot be passed by, with all the power of enthusiasm and a firm resolve; his principles are based on the teaching of Christ, as before him Minter Morgan's, James Pierrepont Greaves 's and Frederick Denison Maurice's had been, but he felt a great sympathy for those who fought for political rights and he repeated again and again that the Chartists were generally misunderstood or misrepresented, but at the same time he preached with the greatest insistence and frank honesty:

"A nobler day is dawning for England, a day of freedom, science, industry, but there will be no true science, without religion, no true industry without the fear of God and love to your fellow-citizens. The sole origin of every right is in a duty fulfilled" [3].

He has laid down these principles in his sociological novels *Alton Locke* and *Yeast.* It is in the first mentioned book that the problem, how to bridge over the gulf between labour and capital has been treated most clearly, and instead of being an abstract reasoning becomes a living force in the person of the tailor-poet, Alton Locke. Alton is a sensitive

1 *The Life of Frederick Denison Maurice.* Chiefly told in his own letters, edited by his son, p. 496.

2 Economic Review, 1893.

3 Cf. J. A. R. Marriot, *Charles Kingsley.*

child, who grows up in one of the squalid streets in the suburbs of London. It is a sort of escape from his sordid life, to stand on Battersea Bridge with the clouds overhead and the glory of the misty Thames before him, a sickly, decrepit Cockney with the light of the setting sun in his eyes, and a hunger and thirst in his soul for the gardens and the meadows and the woods, far out of his reach.

The reality of life is so different from his child-dreams and child-longings: freedom, beauty, honesty, and God's love for all, that it breeds in him a hatred of vulgarity and a revolt against ugliness.

He is brought face to face with the dreadful facts of life in the workroom, where he has to work in the company of a dozen tailors, haggard, untidy, and shoeless, sitting on the ground in a stifling atmosphere; it fills him with disgust, to see the miserable conditions, in which they have to work, but more still, to hear their vulgar language and to get a notion of the bitterness of their hearts.

He feels strangely drawn to Crossthwaite, who is called by the others a Chartist. For the boy that term is synonymous with a wicked rascal, and yet, when their eyes meet, he knows he has found a guide in life.

Soon he is to find his first friend in the person of Sandy Mackaye, an honest Scotchman, who owns a second-hand bookshop. Alton has discovered another source of beauty in the world of books; day after day Mackaye notices the boy reading a copy taken from the outside shelves, with an absorption so great that he is unaware of the reality of London street-life, and so much touched by the adventures and sorrows of his hero that he spoils the pages with his tears.

His thirst for knowledge drives him into disobedience to his mother, but the more he reads, the more his ambition grows to educate himself and to rise in the world. His happiness is spoilt, however, by a feeling of shame about his secrecy and half-heartedness and it is almost a relief to him to be found by his mother, one morning at four o'clock, stitching on his bed, with a Virgil open before him.

Now a feeling of loneliness enters into his soul; he has lost his friend, he is suspected by his mother, he is exhausted by the strain of living two lives and in him there is born a bitter envy of the young men of the upper classes, who do not come to their studies with a tired body and a brain worn out by fatigue; the burning thought arises in him, that fate treats him unjustly and his heart is full of bitter grudgings against those who are more favoured than himself; it sours and maddens him to think that, if he would only desert his class, the world would applaud him, as a rising genius. The struggle between his duty to his mother and his duty to himself ends in a break with home and his return to Mackaye.

After a time the beauty of colour has a great fascination for him and it happens, when he is earnestly gazing at Guido's St. Sebastian that he is roused by a voice and dazzled by the beauty of a human face.

That day he calls the turning-point in his existence, and indeed, the lovely vision becomes the lode-star of all his thoughts. There is an agony of longing in him, to see her again, and his bitterness increases, when he realizes how far she is above him, because he lacks the refinement of her class.

Again he leads two lives, one mechanical and outward, full of revolt and the desire to fight for the Cause of the Chartists, the other, inward and imaginative, full of beauty and longing. He writes a poem about the lone Pacific World, but then Mackaye points out to him that it is his real vocation to be the People's Poet, to look at the naked facts simply and faithfully. Mackaye shows him the terrible sufferings of the poor and the horrors of the Sweating-system [1] and they do their work upon him. Still, it is not all darkness in his soul; his sense of beauty gives it some relieving touches, as he says himself: "If I had to tell the gay ones above of the gloom around me, I had also to go forth into the sunshine, to bring home, if it were but a wild-flower garland to those that sit in darkness and the shadow of death" [2]. In this spirit he writes his Songs of the Highways.

In his outward life the evils of the sweating-system become more and more a reality to him, as he sees the effect on his fellow-workers; he becomes a Chartist, heart and soul; he believes in the Charter as a means to glorious ends, the path to reforms, social, legal, sanatory and educational. When afterwards he looks back to that time, he exclaims: "Fool that I was; it was within, rather than without, that I needed reform!" [3]

In his inward life there is the ambition to have his poems printed, and at the advice of Mackaye he goes to Cambridge to ask for his cousin's help. One glorious morning at the end of May he sets out on his walk to Cambridge, his soul full of exultation, when his child-dream of beauty and freedom becomes a reality: "the hills quivering in the green haze, above the skylarks, pouring out their souls in melody" [4], the poet in him in touch with Nature, listening to the stillness — but then all at once, there is the tailor's shop and the Charter and the starvation and the oppression and he is ashamed of his selfishness. Now he is not bitter or envious; he feels that this is a beauty that should be open to all, but at the same time he asks himself the question: "Shall I grudge simple happiness to the few, because it is as yet, alas, impossible for the many?" [5]

[1] *Alton Locke,* Ch. VIII.
[2] id., Ch. IX.
[3] id., Ch. X.
[4] id., Ch. XI.
[5] id., Ch. XI

He blames himself that he is too proud and too reserved to speak some kind words to a sportsman and his family, and knows that he has no right to complain, as long as he does nothing himself to bridge over the artificial gulf between the class of the well to-do and his own.

He arrives at Cambridge and is impressed by its beauty first; then he envies the students, who enjoy work as well as play, but he wants to keep his independence and his proud conviction of being the People's Poet; and yet it is here at Cambridge that the temptation comes to him which leads to the real turning-point in his life. It is not only his love for Lillian, it is also his envy of the privileged classes, and his pride that cannot bear being slighted, that bring about his fall and make him a coward.

When his patron, Dean Winnstay, advises him to give up the bitter tone against the higher classes and to avoid politics, he consents to have his poems published without the verses that expressed his warmest enthusiasm and most ardent defence of the Cause; this is the real crisis in his life; he has been too half-hearted to stand up for the working-men and to expose their wrongs; it is an offence, not only against his fellow-workers, but an offence against the best that is in him.

He finds favour in the eyes of all, except one, Eleanor, the dark lady, whom he considers his enemy; he is convinced that she wants to separate him from Lillian, and for a moment suspects her of jealousy.

His cousin seems particularly pleased with him and lends him money, to enable him to appear in public as one of them; in his hurry to rise, Alton is going fast down-hill. He has lost his simplicity of mind and is tortured by pangs of conscience.

Coming back to the old life in London, he is painfully

struck by the great contrast between the luxury of the few and the misery of the many, and troubled by remorse at the death of his mother, there is only Mackaye to cling to.

He has no time to wait for inspiration, he must earn money at al costs, to pay his debt, and he becomes a hack-writer, and hates the thought of his being so. In sheer envy and bitterness, he speaks evil and rejoices in evil; it is as if he tries in his execrations to make up for his desertion of his fellow-workers; he endeavours to undo the past and gives all the money he has to some miserable tailors out of a sweater's den; he does all he can, to save them, but he is soon disillusioned, when he finds the men return to the dungeon as their own home; he feels he must atone for the past, but the deed has been done, and he will bear its consequence: it is not only that it has put an end to his quiet of mind, but it brings upon him a fierce attack in the Chartist paper and he smarts at the harsh one-sided jugdment. But the worst moment for him is perhaps, when full of indignation he says to Mackaye that he must explain and the simple-minded old man only asks: "Can ye do that same, laddie?"

He must show that the Cause is as dear to him as ever, and he offers to go to D., the cathedral town, where he has gone through the crisis in his life, in order to see after the poor, starving labourers. He is so much touched by the misery of these desperate men and women that he speaks out freely and is not able to hold them in hand; again he has to bear the consequences; he is accused of being the leader of the rioters and is condemned to three years' imprisonment.

In the loneliness of prison-life the old aspirations for knowledge come back to him and he fills the time with reading and educating himself, but at moments his longing for freedom is so great that he wants to die rather than be shut up; he is wounded to the quick when the recollection of the trial comes over him and he sees the beautiful face of Lillian before him, gay and laughing, without a thought for him in his utmost need.

At last he finds rest in the thought: "Society has cast me off, and in casting me off, it has sent me off to my own people, where I should have stayed from the beginning."

After his release one trouble follows the other: first the disillusioning day of the 10th of April 1848, bringing the failure of the Charter, then the news that his cousin is to marry Lillian, and worst of all the feeling that he has lost his strength of will and his self-control in the fight with his cousin. He does not believe in himself any more and one terrible night, standing on Waterloo Bridge, the temptation comes to him to throw himself over the parapet and put an end to all, and it is only the despair of a fellow-worker, the thought that some one wants him, that saves him from suicide.

In the terrible home of Jemmy Downes [1], he catches a bad fever and for a long time he is unconscious of what happens to him. In his mystic dream he hears a voice and he believes it is Lillian's voice, but waking up, he finds it is Eleanor, who speaks the words: "You have learned what it is to be a man."

Suffering has taught Eleanor that it is her duty to assist her poorer sisters; she has enabled them to work in better conditions, to co-operate and share the earnings among themselves, and she helps Alton to believe in life and in the future again; she teaches him the beauty of enfranchised and fraternal labour, not done by mere men, but by inheritors of the Kingdom of Heaven, that worth does not consist in property, but in the grace of God.

It is of the greatest importance, she says, that the workmen should show themselves worthy of association and it is only

[1] Alton Locke, Ch. XXXV.

by co-operation of all the members of a body that any one member can fulfil its calling in health and freedom.

In utter silence Alton listens to the serious woman, who has been his guardian-angel all through and who works greater miracles in him than Lillian with her beauty has ever been able to. He is no longer under Lillian's spell, not even when he hears she is free, his cousin having died of typhoid-fever caused by a new coat made in a sweater's den, a victim "to the devilish buy-cheap and sell-dear commercialism" [1].

He is full of enthusiasm to be a fighter in the Holy War against social abuses, to overcome the fiend of competition and he believes that the failure of Chartism has awakened a new spirit in high as well as in low. He wants to live for his brothers with patience, made perfect through suffering, but it is not to be.

He dies on the boat that is to take him and Crossthwaite to the Texas and his last words are an encouragement to the fighters in the Holy War: "Face your game and play it."

In Alton Locke's character we can trace Kingsley's belief, that the workers should associate themselves, not in envy of their privileged brothers, but in the spirit of Love, to find beauty in Freedom, Equality and Brotherhood, not by assistance from without, but by the help of the Spirit working in each. The book ends in a hopeful tone, when Crossthwaite states it as his wish to give his small aid in that fraternal union of all classes, which is surely, though slowly, spreading in his motherland.

In Alton Locke we have the story not so much of a conversion as of the hero's return to his native sphere, after a time of trial and temptation, the sphere of freedom, beauty, honesty and God's love for all.

Though *Alton Locke* (1850) was written some five years

[1] cf. Parson Lot, *Cheap clothes and nasty.*

earlier than *Hard Times* and *North and South,* I have treated it last of all, because it forms more or less a link between this period 1830—1866 and the following 1880—1900 in its insistence on co-operation and association of the workers themselves.

Moreover it will become evident that there are some points of resemblance between this novel and George Eliot's sociological novel: *Felix Holt.*

Felix Holt has often been classed as a political novel [1], but I think that the subtitle, *the Radical* has suggested the idea rather than a close examination of the book. I quite agree with A. W. Ward, that it should have a place among the sociological novels of the second period, though it was written more than a decade after the books mentioned above. In its teaching it is closely connected with Charles Kingsley's novel, finding the secret of true reform in "the resolve of the masses to learn and think and act for themselves" [2].

The elections in the provincial town of Treby Magna form the background, against which the two principal characters Felix Holt and Esther Lyon stand out; the fact that there is but a loose connection between the characters and the social life of their time, explains why *Felix Holt* cannot be reckoned among George Eliot's best works; in a way she accounts for this defect, when she says:

"This history is chiefly concerned with the private life of a few men and women, but there is no private life which has not been determined by a wider public life."

On the other hand she makes us see, how Felix Holt in his individual life hoped to set an example of honest work done faithfully in a simple sphere of life thus, influencing for the good, a wider public life.

[1] Cf. M. E. Speare, *The Political Novel,* Ch. VIII.

[2] Cf. Cambridge History of English Literature, Vol. XIII, Ch. XI.

Felix Holt has found that the best path in life for him is to give up a life of comparative luxury, since it is obtained by dishonest means. His father has left him the secret of a patent medicine, which he knows to be a fraud and though his mother has to bear the consequences as well as himself, he decides to be a workman among his own people, rather than be ashamed of himself.

Moreover, a life of luxury has no attraction for Felix; he sees nothing but unnaturalness in it, and, when he meets Esther Lyon, he dislikes her for her refined tastes and tells her with brusque openness that "a fine lady is a squirrel-headed thing, with small airs and small notions."

We find the two qualities that were to George Eliot the end of all aspirations, namely self-sacrificing, helpful love and renunciation, embodied in Felix from the beginning and in Esther only after a long process of growth and battle.

Esther is the daughter of an Independent minister, who has placed herself on a pedestal, from where she looks down upon the simple people about her. "She had a little code of her own, by which she secretly condemned or sanctioned all things and persons. And she was well satisfied with herself for her fastidious taste, never doubting that hers was the highest standard."

She thinks herself far superior to her father, the simple-minded, straight-forward man, who has a feeling of awe in the company of his beautiful daughter; it is true, she respects the purity of his character, but then, there is something ridiculous in his untidy appearance, and if there is anything that Esther hates, it is to be laughed at in public. She cannot bear to be treated, as if her existence was of no importance in the world, and she longs for admiration and applause.

Centred as she is on her own likings and tastes, she has no eyes for the difficulties of others, and not the slightest idea that there can be something wanting in her. And so it is all the harder for her, when Felix Holt, instead of admiring her, constantly criticizes her; it makes her angry that he behaves as if he is immeasurably her superior, because it shakes her in her self-content; but, what vexes her most of all is that she has a secret consciousness that he is her superior.

This is the beginning of an inward struggle; something has been awakened in her, a doubt and uncertainty that are to disturb the even tenor of her life.

Though his bitter words hurt her, she cares about his opinion and is pleased at the slightest sign of appreciation, when he tells her that "she has too much understanding to add one more to the women who hinder men's lives from having any nobleness in them". She begins to understand that her father's life is lonely and her sympathy may be a help to him.

Her kind words are a revelation to him and she is struck by the look in his eyes, when he says: "You have become the image of your mother."

Again and again her pride rebels against the idea of submission to another and she tries to keep Felix at a distance and to assure herself that it is not his doing and that his criticism is of no consequence to her. Up to now her life has been one of proud, self-willed complacency, and the satisfaction she finds in forgetting self for a moment, in order to make this world a better place for her father, is not sufficient to make up for the loss of self-confidence.

Felix is greatly interested in her, but in his life there is no place for her; his work is cut out for him: showing the way to others, happy in being able to contribute to the happiness of his fellow-workers, however little that may be. He says:

"Where great things can 't happen, I care for very small things, such as will never be known beyond a few garrets and workshops. I will try to make life less bitter for a few within my reach." His work is all in all to him and he is not going to let a fine lady have any influence on his life.

When we compare the characters of Alton Locke and Felix Holt, we find that both are strong natures, conscious of the necessity to devote the best that is in them to the Cause of the workers, but in Alton Locke there is far more restlessness and impatience than in Felix Holt; Alton is brought into actual contact with the misery of the workman, whereas Felix is living up to his ideals, without fighting the enemy hand to hand.

In the life of both, love comes as a great temptation, but whereas Alton renounces his principles, Felix does not allow his personal happiness to interfere with his vocation. He is deeply touched by the change in Esther, but as long as she does not belong to his class, he can only feel friendship for her. At the critical moment of being put in the position of leader of a riotous crowd, Alton loses his self-control and brings misery over others, as well as over himself, Felix faces the circumstances, and, seeing that he has not the power to meet them, he tries to prevent the worst consequences to others, though he is conscious that he exposes himself to the greatest danger. In spite of the fact that Felix kills one of the constables, we feel that Felix is superior to the situation, while Alton is carried along against his will.

Alton's message to his fellow-workers is: "Claim your rights, but know that your greatest happiness lies within you," whereas Felix, though he is not against political reforms, does not see or plead the workers' need of them and wants to stand up for the lot of the handicraftsman as a good lot, in which a man may be better trained to all the best functions of his nature.

When Felix after the riot is in prison, circumstances seem to widen the gulf between Esther and him; the truth comes to light that she is not Mr. Lyon's daughter, but that she is entitled to a place of rank and fortune, for which she has been longing all her life; she is invited to stay at Transome Court and Harold Transome is quite prepared to marry her. It seems that her day-dreams have come true at last; she is flattered that every one considers her fit for the high position that is awaiting her, but somehow the glamour is gone and the new life, instead of being a gain, seems a loss and a disenchantment to her.

The temptation has not lost all its force though; it would be so easy, to let herself go, to accept the homage of Harold Transome, to believe that this is the real solution of the problem of her lot; and yet, there is something dull in this ease, in the absence of high ambitions.

In this state of conflict, some words that she speaks without any forethought, reveal her inner being to herself. It is when Harold Transome promises to do whatever he can for that eccentric young man, Felix Holt, that she says without flinching: "If it is eccentricity to be very much better than other men, he is certainly eccentric; and fanatical too, if it is fanatical to renounce all small selfish motives for the sake of a great and unselfish one." There is now only one fear in her heart, the fear that the life of high endeavour may prove a delusion.

"It was what the dread of a pilgrim might be, who has it whispered to him, that the holy places are a delusion, or that he will see them with a soul unstirred and unbelieving" [1]. But after speaking to Felix in prison, all her doubts are silenced.

The crisis in her life is at hand; at Felix's trial she stands at the parting of the ways. Surrounded by al the people whose opinion she has valued above everything, and whose ridicule has damped all that is noble in her, she takes fate

[1] *Felix Holt,* Ch. XLV.

into her own hands and bravely speaks up for Felix, telling that his intentions before the riot were to calm the people and to prevent a disturbance. And, though at first it seems as if her words have no effect and Felix is sentenced to four years' imprisonment, her moral courage has impressed the gentry of Treby Magna to such a degree, that by their influence a release is obtained for Felix Holt.

Esther, who up to this time has been leaning on others, finds that she is able to lift and strengthen those weaker than herself. With her fine feeling she knows how to comfort Mrs. Transome, and reconcile Harold to his mother.

She has chosen her path and gives up her claim to the estate of the Transomes.

George Eliot has given in the character of Esther, what she has done before in many of her heroines, the happiness that grows out of the choice of a life of privation and renunciation of what seems to her empty luxury. We cannot help thinking that in Felix Holt she has given us another Frank Henley [1], though a modern one, and that it is more for the sake of his message than for the sake of his personality that we are interested in him.

That message he wants to bring to all workers as the thing that they want most of all: to find their happiness in their own station in life, doing their little share for the good of all.

When we consider the novelists of this period, we find that in spite of the fact that they are fully aware of the urgency of the social needs, they have a firm belief in the remedies that they suggest; Dickens and Mrs. Gaskell in a better understanding between master and man, brought about by a more intimate knowledge and unselfish love; Kingsley in an association and co-operation of the workers, based

[1] Cf. *Anna St. Ives.*

on the teaching of Christ, and George Eliot in the renunciation of all selfish desires. This confidence becomes evident in the conversion that takes place in the lives of their heroes and heroines.

There is no despondence, no sense of failure, but a looking forward to a better future and a hopeful trust in man, guided by the Spirit of Love.

Introduction to Chapters III, IV, V

Ideas of the Third Period
The Sociological Novel, influenced by the Rise of Democracy

Just as in the sociological novel of the second Period there is a reaction against the spirit of rationalism that we find in the revolutionary novel of the first Period, so in the sociological novel of the third Period there is a protest against the trustful confidence and belief in the future that is to be found in the humanitarian novel of the second Period.

In the last two decades of the nineteenth century the aspect of society has changed a good deal [1]. A great many of the political rights that the Chartists had claimed, have been obtained, but the expectations that the gulf between the classes would be bridged over, have proved false, and instead of a reconciliation and a better understanding that the social reformers had hoped to bring about, there is only a separation so great that it has led to a class-war. "This *is* a class war; we mean to break down competition and to substitute universal organisation and co-operation, with our social creed as our only religion, the scientific organisation of labour and the universal brotherhood of man" [2].

Increase of want with increase of wealth goes on at a more rapid rate in the later than in the earlier years of the nineteenth century, as A. R. Wallace says in *The Wonderful Century:* "One of the most prominent features of the nineteenth

[1] Cf. J. H. Rose, *The Rise of Democracy.*

[2] Cf. H. M. Hyndman and W. Morris, *A. Summary of the Principles of Socialism.*

century has been the enormous growth of wealth, without any corresponding increase in the well-being of the whole people: while there is ample evidence to show that the number of the very poor — of those existing with a minimum of the bare necessities of life — has enormously increased."

Whereas in the first Period the solution of the social problem was expected from a reliance on truth and reason, in the second Period from fellow-feeling and association in a spirit of Christian love, which both would lead to acts of individual will, the crying social evils of the third Period necessitate a social evolution in which the whole of society is to play a part. The gulf between the proletariate and the landlord and capitalist class has widened more and more, as Ramsay Macdonald says: "Wealth divorced from social responsibility, but held and used purely as a personal possession, has divided society into two great separate kingdoms of rich and poor, each living its own life and very rarely coming into contact with the other"[1]. And everywhere the battle-cry of the Socialists sounds loud: "Brothers unite!"

Meanwhile the great thinkers, Ruskin and Morris have followed the line of attack, started by Carlyle,[2] reiterating his message with the most earnest insistence, that the happiness of man is to be found in seeking "not greater wealth, but simpler pleasure, not higher fortune, but deeper felicity, making the first of possessions, self-possession, and honouring themselves in the harmless pride and calm pursuits of peace."[3] Carlyle's gospel: "Know thy work", is preached in a new form by Morris: "Find joy in thy work."

What Morris demanded was, freedom and beauty, fellowship and joy in creative work; his life was a revolt against the

[1] Cf. Ramsay Macdonald, *The Socialist Movement,* p. 42.
[2] Cf. A. Compton-Rickett, *W. Morris,* Ch. XIV.
[3] Cf. Ruskin, *Unto this Last,* Essay IV.

sordidness, misery and ugliness of a cramped existence [1].

Ardent socialist as he was, he knew that political rights should be a means and not an end in themselves; what was needed over and above the blessing of work in freedom and fellowship was: "a revolution in the spirit of the workers which should back up all desire of change with intelligence, courage and power. Intelligence enough to conceive, courage enough to will, power enough to compel" [2].

His own experience made him desire that the happiness he had found in the sense of being useful in the world, not being like plants thrust into the earth, which cannot turn this way or that, but as the wind blows them; with the knowledge of what he wanted and the will to find it, the happiness and the joy in work, done with all the power that was in him, should be sought by others, and that no other work should be done than the work worth doing.

Now the question arises: "Which of these ideas are prominent in the novels, written by George Gissing, Mrs. Humphry Ward, William Hale White, Arthur Morrison and Richard Whiteing, and the answer must be that none of them give an illustration of any social creed; but that in all of them we find the spirit of democracy, the conscioussness of the deep gulf separating rich and poor, and in most of them a tone of despondence and a sense of failure.

The novel of purpose, giving at least a hint of a solution of the social problem has made place for the novel of problem [3], searching for the hidden disease, laying bare the wounds, and showing the evils with the honesty of realism. Though no remedies are given, their mission seems to come to us in the battle-cry that they send forth: "Awake!"

[1] Cf. J. Bruce Glasier, *W. Morris.*

[2] Cf. Holbrook Jackson, *William Morris.*

[3] Cf. F. H. Stoddard, *The Evolution of the English Novel.*

The messages of Ruskin and Morris are not to be found so easily as the preaching of Carlyle in the sociological novels of the second period, but, scattered as these messages are, they will be seen to be the life-giving spirit in the characters, drawn by Gissing and his contemporaries. We find in their novels the same leading thoughts as in the novels of the first and the second period.

Dissatisfaction with the existing conditions, in the endeavour to give to each man a life worth having and work worth doing.

A longing to return to Nature, in the joy in simple pleasure, in the love of Nature and in the need of fellowship and helpful influencc.

The necessity of simplification as regards social life in the consciousness that the luxury and wealth of the few can only be had at the expense of the misery of the many.

Chapter III

The Sociological Novel by George R. Gissing and Mrs. Humphry Ward — A contrast

George Robert Gissing has often been called the apostle of pessimism, and in truth, the reading of his novels leaves a sense of depression caused by the insight they give us into the joyless existence of thousands and thousands of our fellow-beings; but, looking beneath the surface, we shall find that Gissing does not really preach pessimism; in many of his heroes and heroines we find a courage to face life, in spite of the frustration of their expectations, or at least the resolution to fight it out to the end.

May Yates has pointed out that there is such a thing as a "Gissing legend" [1], but, though it may be true that he only suffered real poverty when writing his first novel, and that he was not a social outlaw, it cannot be denied that his life was a hard one, that the abrupt ending of his studies at the age of eighteen was a heavy blow to his ambition and that he was disillusioned in his first marriage as well as in the second and that he, the man who regarded love and art as the moving principles of life [2], had to fight his way amidst the greatest vulgarity of London back-streets. He spoke from experience, when he said of one of his heroes: "To stab the root of a young tree, to hang crushing burdens upon it, to rend off its early branches, that is not the treatment likely to result in growth such as nature purposed."

[1] May Yates, *George Gissing*, p. 3.

[2] Cf. Edwin Björkman, *Voices of To-morrow*.

Swinnerton [1] says that ambition poisoned his life, but, if it was the ambition to uphold his ideal of doing no other work than that chosen as the best and to refuse to do any work that he thought beneath him, we cannot help thinking that though this ambition may have spoilt his worldly prospects, it can never have poisoned his inner life.

Fighting as he was against adverse circumstances, we can understand his bitterness and revolt at times. His attidude through life, Seccombe says, was "that of a man who, having set out on his career with the understanding that a second-class ticket is to be provided, allows himself to be unceremoniously hustled into the rough and tumble of a noisy third" [2].

His life among the poor gave him an intimate knowledge of their ways and thoughts, and though he lacks the humour of Dickens, and the fellow-feeling for them as a class, he is certainly touched by the pathos of their existence and shows us, perhaps better than Dickens could, the heroic struggle and steadfast faith of some of them.

What we see in Gissing's life, we find again in his characters, the conflict between temperament and environment. Gissing, of whom Austin Harrison says: "By nature he was made for the life of tranquillity and meditation, for cultured leisure and repose" [3], had to toil and struggle and did not find his home of beauty and love before the last few years of his life.

It gives one a sense of satisfaction, to read the letters he wrote to his friend Edward Clodd [4] in that peaceful period of his life, in which bitterness and loneliness be-

[1] Cf. Fr. Swinnerton, *G. Gissing.*

[2] Cf. Thomas Seccombe, *The Work of George Gissing.*

[3] Cf. Austin Harrison, *Nineteenth Century,* 1906.

[4] *Letters to Edward Clodd.* London. Printed for Thomas J. Wise, Hampstead N. W. Edition limited to Thirty Copies.

longed to the past, and I cannot refrain from quoting some lines from them, explaining as they do, even better than *The Ryecroft Papers* (1903) that at the bottom of his heart Gissing was not a pessimist.

A letter, dated April 27th 1900, says:

"Impossible to tell you, how I enjoyed my stay in your house. The utter restfulness of it. It has done me good, body and mind. — We [1] were at a concert, given by Delaborde, one of the finest of pianists. I, who am no friend of public entertainments, came back, glad in heart and mind."

And another, dated March 1st 1902:

"Above all, it is the existence of natural beauty which haunts my thought. I can, for a time forget the world's horrors, I can never forget the flower by the wayside and the sun falling in the west."

It was perhaps his love of beauty and hatred of vulgarity that incited him to show with all the power of his realism, the degrading influence of poverty and to lay the social problem before us in the pathetic lives of his characters, "while with a profounder knowledge than Ruskin, Carlyle or Morris had, when they revolted against its ugliness, Gissing pictured the world of poverty, its streets and purlieus and dens, the whole atmosphere of it, squalid and without a vestige of beauty" [2].

Besides the degrading influence of poverty, Gissing shows the necessity of realizing that between the educated and the uneducated there is a barrier, dividing them into two classes, which makes it impossible for each of them to understand the motives of the other's actions; he makes us see what the influence of suddenly acquired wealth is on the character of the uneducated man, coming into close con-

[1] Gissing and Gabrielle.

[2] Cambridge History of English Literature, Vol. XIII, Ch. 14.

tact with the educated classes. A very clear example of this influence he gives us in his novel *Demos.* (1886).

The two characters, illustrating his views are Adela Waltham and Richard Mutimer.

Adela in her quiet home-life, is happy in her religious views, sitting in her little room, "a nest of purity and neatness", spending her time in illustrating a text of Scripture. Yet there is a latent strength in her, which comes out now and then, when she refuses to read the practical books her Radical-minded brother wants to give her. She has a complete trust in her mother, she is young and frank, without self-conceit, and only affirmative in her opinions, when religion is the topic of conversation. There is something narrow in her Puritan outlook on life, but she has an instinct of justice, which saves her from harshness and conventionality and which makes her see another's point, even if she disagrees with him.

She is in love with Hubert Eldon and fully believes in him, with his openness of look, his tone of pleasant directness, and it comes to her as a great shock, to hear her mother speak about the dissipation of that bad young man in Paris; she does not doubt her mother's accusation for a moment; this world of vice and sin is so far from her own horizon that it only hurts her to the quick, to know Hubert is capable of doing mean things, and that she is ashamed to acknowledge to herself that she loves him still.

The Paris episode has cost Hubert Eldon his inheritance; Mr. Mutimer has destroyed his will in favour of Hubert, and the Wanley Estate is conferred on a relation of old Mr. Mutimer's, an ardent Socialist in London. Richard Mutimer, when we meet him for the first time, makes an impression of strength and energy; he is full of enthusiasm for the Cause of the Workman, absorbed in his schemes, taken up by his speeches for the Union to such a degree that there is something detached in his behaviour at home, and even to Emma, the working-girl to whom he is engaged. He loves his mother, and spoils his sister, whom they call the Princess, but his propaganda goes before everything else.

He has educated himself and bought books for every spare penny and the library he possesses, represents his mental sphere. Every book is either for or against something, every pamphlet contains an opinion that may be useful to him in his Socialist propaganda, but English Literature is to him a sealed volume; poetry he scarcely knows by name. He feels no other emotion than the heat of the fight against oppression; he is honest to himself and to others, but there is in him a vein of vanity which makes him keen on applause and proud of his influence as an orator.

The first effect that the suddenly acquired wealth has on this young enthusiast, fighting for a glorious end, is that it attacks him in his weak point, his vanity. It is not so much that he is pleased to be rich and have a life of luxury; he has spent too great a part of his life in attacking the evils of wealth, but foremost in his thoughts is the idea that he will be the glorified representative of his class. He will show how a self-taught working-man conceives the duties and privileges of wealth, his gospel will be trumpeted over the land.

The money will enable him to fight for the Cause better than ever before; he has not the slightest idea of deserting his class and is happy, when he can tell Emma that those possessions are his and hers, and that a good life is coming now. He is hurt, that his enthusiasm finds no response, when his mother, full of apprehension of the danger, says: "It is bad news," and Emma in her quiet way answers: "I never thought about money; it was quite enough to be your wife."

In his imagination Richard Mutimer builds his future: the

mines at Wanley wil be the basis of great industrial undertakings; it will be a settlement conducted on Socialist principles; the profits will benefit no individual, but the Cause. He discusses his plans with the Editor of the Fiery Cross, and he is not altogether satisfied, when in the Union's weekly organ, there is only a brief paragraph about the enterprise, and Richard Mutimer's name is not mentioned.

It is gratifying to his vanity, however, when he is warmly applauded by his comrades, and he ends his speech with the words: "I shall still be of the people and with the people. I'll use every opportunity that's given me to uphold the cause of the poor and downtrodden against the rich and selfish and luxurious."

Full of enthusiasm and with a firm confidence in his plan he begins his work at Wanley and very soon circumstances bring Richard Mutimer and Adela Waltham together. In Richard's mind the comparison arises between Adela with all the refined manners of a lady and Emma with her simple ways and as time goes on, it seems as if Emma is drifting far from him, or he from her. More and more seldom can he find time to visit his relations or write to Emma. It is a relief to him that she puts off the date of the marriage, because of her sister's illness.

The power of his position is a glory to Richard; to receive honoured guests, to be the central figure is all that he desires. He becomes an easy prey to the flattery of Mr. Rodman, his right-hand man in the undertaking, and Mr. Keene, a journalist, whom in his poorer days he had not thought quite good enough for his sister. Mr. Keene has written an article in the provincial paper, the Belwick Chronicle under the heading: "Men of the Day", with loud praises of Richard Mutimer, and from that time Richard considers him as a friend. Mutimer's only ambition now is to have "a lady" for his wife, and as Adela's beauty appeals to him, he sees her as the future mistress of Wanley.

There is a struggle in him, when he thinks of the hard-working girl in London, with her steadfast faith in him, but he suffers himself to be captured by the illusion that she is a clog on him and that he is the real sufferer. His mother's letter, summoning him to come and marry Emma, makes him angry, and when Emma herself writes to thank him for the money and in the envelope he finds a paper with a few touching lines, written by Jane's sister, who is on the point of death, his only feeling is that there must be an end to this suspense; he throws Emma's letter into the fire and, longing for a decision, he goes straight to Adela's house and proposes to her.

He has chosen the path where his vanity has led him and there is no returning; he persuades his sister to tell his mother and Emma, and though he hopes he has made it perfectly clear to her, he will never be the same in her eyes.

For Adela the weeks before Richard's definite proposal have also been a time of great struggle.

At their first meeting she has felt a sort of irritation against him; it is a real sorrow to her to see the splendid piece of Nature spoiled by the settlement in the valley, but her sense of justice makes her see that there is some good in his devotion to an unselfish cause, and though her class-instinct is against him, she strives against her feelings that he is not a perfect gentleman. It hurts her that her mother encourages Mr. Mutimer's advances; her mind is making itself free of the bonds of youth; she begins to criticize her mother, and there is something painful in it as their lives are drifting apart. It seems to her that life can never be so sunny as before: she cannot forget her love for Hubert Eldon and yet she is unwilling to cause sorrow to her mother. And in the end there are two things that make her accept the proposal: her pride, which is wounded that Hubert should have considered her of so little account, and her religious hopes to plead with Mr. Mutimer and bring him to the truth.

She is strengthened in her resolve by a bit of gossip in the provincial paper, announcing Hubert's marriage with a French actress.

It appears to her a duty now to be led by her mother and to marry Mutimer; so she begins her new life with an ascetic sternness; all the same there is something broken in her and there is a distinct change in her manners, a sort of cold dignity; and even in her tone there is something authoritative, as if she felt it needful to remind herself that she is happy because she is useful.

She begins to study hard, because it is not enough for her to say to others: "All Christians ought to be socialists;" she wants to understand her husband's ideas and it is her secret wish to use her knowledge as a means of converting him. It seems as if his intellectual sphere is going to be hers, but in reality their natures are so far apart from each other, so incompatible that they must needs clash.

At a tea-party that Adela gives to the children of New Wanley, the socialist settlement, two little ones have come to implore Mrs Mutimer's interference. Their father has been dismissed by Richard on the ground of drunkenness and impudence. Adela pleads with him to forgive the offence and while she is speaking, the vague fear becomes a certainty that it is not only for the sake of principle, that Richard does not yield. The words: "my authority" make her understand her husband's motives; she sees as something dreadful that his work has nothing noble in it, if it is his vanity that leads him on. It is a bitter disappointment, but her pride enables her to hide it from others; she tries, to silence her own doubts of his honesty, when she hears in a letter about his behaviour to Emma, for, if that were true, there would be nothing to cling to.

Richard's ambition after a time aims at being a Member of Parliament, being known as an advocate of the Cause throughout the country; now the frustration of these hopes brings out all his worst qualities, and Adela, seeing him come towards her in his drunkenness, is fully conscious of the monstrous gulf between them. She is only too glad to get an invitation from Mrs. Westlake, the wife of the Socialist editor; she finds herself once more in a home, where she can breathe freely; it is a time, full of enchantment and beauty to her.

She has promised to bring about a meeting between Mrs. Westlake and Richard's sister, who is now Mrs. Rodman, but she feels again that the gulf is too wide. Richard sees her slip away from him more and more; his jealousy is aroused by meeting Hubert Eldon in Adela's company in London, and he becomes masterful and suspicious, after he has forced her to come home, and all the same, he is in awe of her pure honesty.

The moment that will prove which of the two natures is able to dominate, is near at hand. Adela has found a paper in the family-pew, which proves to be old Mr. Mutimer's testament; the old man's last will must inevitably bring about Richard's ruin and he tries to convince Adela that the good of hundreds of thousands is at stake. But Adela's mind has made itself free and she asks him frankly: "What causes all the misery but dishonesty and selfishness? If you do away with that, you gain all you are working for" [1].

He makes an attempt to frighten her into submission, but her strength of will is greater than his, and she declares that

[1] G. Gissing, *Demos,* Ch. XXIV, p. 294.

she will not hide the secret, if he destroys the will. After that there is nothing for him, but to give in.

In the three weeks that follow the catastrophe Richard's vanity helps him in tiding over the difficulties; the sympathy expressed in letters, in the newspapers and most of all in a letter from a Minister of the Crown are a cause of satisfaction to him; in the closing ceremony of New Wanley Hall he poses as a victim of cruel circumstances and promises that the small legacy left to him, every penny of it, will be used for the furtherance of the Cause.

Adela is not so pleased with herself; suffering has taught her to study herself and she feels that in restoring the estate to its real owner, she has not only been led by a sense of honour, but that her decision has been influenced by her love for Hubert Eldon.

Her pride forbids her to let any ony know that her marriage is an unhappy one; moreover, she is aware that it is she who must shield Richard, even against himself.

In the squalid lodgings in London, life becomes a real torture to her; what oppresses her is not the fear of poverty, but the aversion that is growing in her to her husband's coarse outlook on things, his suspicion, and his cruelty. "She was deficient in the strength of character which will subdue all circumstances; her strength was of the kind that supports endurance rather than breaks a way to freedom. Every day, every hour, is some such tragedy played through, it is the inevitable result of our social state"[1]. By a gift from an unknown Socialist friend, Richard Mutimer is enabled to continue his work, but the first use that he makes of the money is to take a better house and to engage a servant. His thoughts are full of his book: *My work at New Wanley,* which he will have published and spread among the workers. He explains to Adela that

[1] *Demos,* Ch. XXXVIII p. 341.

he will make the East End know him as well as they know any man in England; he has made a plan to attract the attention of the poor: he will save their money for them; as soon as they have trusted him with a hundred pounds, he will add another hundred of his own, that will give him a hold over them. It is against Socialist principles, it is true, but then, he does not care how he makes Socialists, if only he gets them to join the Union.

But luck seems to have deserted Richard, his unknown benefactor dies; his scheme of the workmen's savings threatens to become a failure, and he knows that failure means the loss of his influence and his reputation; that is the reason why he risks the money in an undertaking which he believes to be honest. It all proves to be a swindle and Richard knows that this will be the end of his power over his comrades, unless he can prove that he is innocent.

On the evening of the Socialist meeting Richard is prevented from going because of his sister's disappearance from their house, where she was being nursed; his anxiety about Alice re-awakens in him his old fondness of "the Princess" and he must needs try and find her, whatever may be the consequences to himself. — Adela realizes what these consequences may be, if Richard disappoints the meeting, and her sense of justice overcomes her disgust; she goes to the club and addresses the assembly, declaring that her husband is incapable of doing the horrible thing of which he is accused: robbing his comrades of their savings.

She encourages him to go to Clerkenwell Green, to speak calmly to the people; there he finds only a few supporters and a crowd of enemies; the feeling of the mob is hopelessly against him and when the story is being unearthed, how scandalously Mutimer has treated a poor working-girl, the people get excited to such a degree that all sense of order is lost; Demos is having his way — Richard is pursued and wounded and dies with the bitter sense of failure: "That's the People, that is! I deserve killing, fool that I am, if only for the lying good I've said of them" [1].

Adela does all she can, to clear her husband's honour after his death; it is an act of justice she owes to him. And though pride keeps her apart for a time from the man whom she has loved all her life, she finds happiness at last in her natural sphere.

In *Demos* Gissing is said to have given the failure of Socialism, and Richard Mutimer as a type of the Socialist Leaders, and truly we may take for granted that at the time when Gissing wrote *Demos,* he saw no hopes in the work done by the Socialist parties, which lacked unity of purpose [2], but we must not forget that the tragedy in *Demos* is not one owing to circumstances, but to character.

The words of the Vicar, Mr. Wyvern: "They are not themselves of pure and exalted character; they cannot ennoble others" [3] voice Gissing's view of the Social question, he has embodied this view in the character of Richard Mutimer, but though his tone may be far from hopeful, still there is a hint here and there to show that Gissing sees a faint light in the darkness, in Adela's words to her husband: "If you do away with dishonesty and selfishness, you gain all you are working for" and in the comfort that Adela found in "the truth that there is a work in the cause of humanity other than that which goes on so clamorously in lecture-halls and at street corners — the work of those whose soul is taken captive of loveliness, who pursue the spiritual ideal, apart from the world's tumult, and, ever ready to minister in

[1] *Demos,* Ch. XXV, p. 422.

[2] Cf. J. Bruce Glasier, *William Morris,* Ch. II.

[3] *Demos,* Ch. XXIX, p. 355.

gentle offices, know that they serve best, when nearest home" [1].

In the marriage of Richard and Adela, Gissing has shown an attempt to ignore class-distinctions; Adela had spent years in trying to convince herself that nothing but an unworthy prejudice parted class from class, only to find that the reality of life belied all her theorizing on abstract principles.

The gulf separating the civilized and the uneducated is also the subject of *Thyrza* (1887); and, whereas in *Demos* Gissing has pointed out, how Socialist interference comes to nothing, where nobility of character is lacking, in *Thyrza* he shows the failure of philanthropy, the uselessness of palliatives, the disillusionment of the idealist, Walter Egremont.

Walter's father had begun life as a house-painter, had been very successful, and had left to his son extensive works in Lambeth; Walter often thought with tenderness of the clear-headed and warm-hearted man, but he did not feel the least inclination to continue his father's work. He was far more a thinker than a worker; at times he was disposed to idle dreaming, and his face, when in rest, had a thoughtful, often even a melancholy expression; it was when the social wrongs haunted his mind and a feeling of responsibility made him ask again and again, what part he was to act in the world. He was not in sympathy with those socialists who only considered the material welfare of the working-class; he believed that the time of better wages, shorter hours, and decent homes was coming, but the all-important question for him was: "What are the workmen going to do with these advantages?"

He saw that the tendency of society was to regard it as the end of life to make money and the conviction strengthened in him that no reform would bring about any good, if it was not the outcome of a change in men's minds.

[1] *Demos*, Ch. XXXVI, p. 436.

Egremont was not the philosopher who was blind to the facts of life; with great sadness in his heart he realized that he was unable to deal with the very lowest, "the mud at the bottom of society"; he expected that "only the vast changes to be wrought by time will cleanse that foulness, by destroying the monstrous wrong which produces it" [1], but he believed in a brighter future, even if it must be a remote future, when he said: "There is no way of lifting those poor people out of the mire; if their children's children tread on firm ground, it will be the most we can hope for" [2].

After a time of restlessness and doubt he thought that he had found the solution of the social problem in the spiritual education of the upper artisan and mechanic class; he believed that they would be able to influence those above them, no less than those below, and that the moral power that they had over their fellow-beings would undo the work of half-taught revolutionists.

And, in coming to that conclusion, he had also clearly seen what work was cut out for him personally; by birth he belonged to the artisan class; he had spent his youth among educated people and he often felt as if he belonged to neither; now it occurred to him that he was in a position to be useful as a mediator between the two sections of society.

But it is exactly the fact that he belongs to neither sphere, which is to cause his failure; he is a man who feels at home in the world of books, who prefers solitude to society, who, from the beginning, when he comes into contact with the artisans of Lambeth, is drawn towards Grail, one of the mechanics, who, like himself, is a lonely man by nature and has found his best friends in his books, but he is unable to

[1] *Thyrza*, Ch. II, p. 14.
[2] id., Ch. VIII, p. 92.

understand the mind of the average artisan, and however great his advantages are in his undertaking: his sincerity of purpose, and his youthful enthusiasm, they do not compensate for his lack of strength and perseverance.

It is not that he is over-optimistic, for, when he explains his plans for the first time to his friends, he says: "I don 't know that I am strong enough for such an undertaking, but I feel the desire to try, and I mean to try" [1].

In this mood he begins his work with giving a free course of lectures on English literature; this he only considers as a means of getting on a friendly footing with his audience; when he has attained that, he will be on the way to founding his club of social reformers; he knows that success depends on his personal influence, and he will try and give them the beauty that he has found in Shelley's poems and Ruskin's prose as a blessing in their lives of toil and vulgar recreation.

He is sincere in his ardent hopes for the well-being of others, but even before setting to work, he cannot put aside his personal happiness and thinks a woman's love necessary to have full confidence in himself. When Annabel Newthorpe says she can only give him friendship, but not the love that he wants, his words make it evident that it is not the work for its own sake that is a sacred duty to him: "I shall pursue this work that I have undertaken, because, loving you, I dare not fall below the highest life of which I am capable" [2].

A few months after he has begun his lectures Egremont states to Mrs. Ormonde, the mother of a friend he has lost, that of his hearers Grail is the only man that he is sure of; he has lost one already; his impressions of another have continued to grow unfavourable; a third is a mystery to him; still, he is not discouraged; it is a great satisfaction to

[1] *Thyrza*, Ch. II, p. 15.
[2] id., Ch. II, p. 21.

him, to find a real friend in Grail, and to make him share his enthusiasm. With his help he hopes to reach the others, not knowing that the only impression that he has made upon them, is worded by one of the artisans: "What business has the fellow to have so much time that he does not know what to do with it" [1].

The friendship of Egremont is a source of joy to Grail; though rather late in life, it seems that now the sun has broken through the clouds; instead of spending his time in mechanical work, he will be able to live among his beloved books, for Egremont has offered him the post of librarian in a free library which will be founded in Lambeth among his own people.

His salary is such that without fear of the future he can make a home and realize a long-cherished wish, to call Thyrza his own.

In Thyrza and her sister Gissing has painted two shining figures of loveliness standing out against the sombre background of Lambeth Walk.

When Egremont visits Grail, he envies him, and would give all the money that his father had amassed, if in exchange he could have grown up in a home like Grail's, where he finds refinement without any artificiality. Egremont has been struck by Thyrza's voice, when unexpectedly she came upon him in the library, and still more by her uncommon beauty; to Thyrza the meeting has been a revelation of that brighter world of her daydreams, and very soon she gets better acquainted with Egremont's sphere of life, when she pays a visit to Mrs Ormonde, who takes convalescent children into her home at Eastbourne, by chance Thyrza has been asked to take a little girl there; she has never been far away from Lambeth and the downs and

[1] *Thyrza,* Ch. IV, p. 74.

the sea are a very wonderland to her; the vision of the illimitable sea makes her feel one with the Infinite, and the short space of time, spent in the new beauty and glory is decisive for her future. "You have watched with interest some close-folded bud; one day all promise is shut within those delicate sepals, and on the next, for the fulness of time has come, you find the very flower with its glow and its perfume. So it sometimes happens that a human soul finds its season, and at a touch expands to wonderful new life" [1].

Thyrza begins to understand her own mind, and after meeting Egremont again at the library, after his request to speak to him, as to a friend, she becomes aware, that the calm she felt in Grail's affection has come to an end, and has made place for a yearning for Egremont's love.

Egremont, who had hoped that his plans for the workers would form a task for life which would give him satisfaction and content, feels how the old unrest has come over him again, and how the sympathy for Thyrza has ripened into a great passion.

Both Egremont and Thyrza realize that duty requires them to leave their deepest thoughts without expression; their foremost idea is to spare Grail; neither at the time takes into account the fatal gulf that separates his class from hers.

Egremont on purpose avoids meeting Thyrza; he makes up his mind to leave London and not to come back before the marriage of Grail and Thyrza has taken place; but it is all in vain, for Thyrza, once having seen the truth, knows that she must live up to it; she feels that she cannot possibly make Grail happy and she writes a letter to her sister to explain all. She has broken with her past and even Lydia must not know her address.

[1] *Thyrza*, Ch. XVI, p. 189.

There are only few persons who know Egremont well enough not to blame him; appearances are dead against him and it hurts him to be cut by people who before treated him with respect. The greater is the relief that Grail believes in his honesty, but it does not alter the fact, that they can never be on terms of intimacy again, that Grail cannot accept the post of librarian, and that Egremont has lost what little influence he may have had on the people in Lambeth. The work that was to be his task for life, has come to a sudden end. The only person who is able to understand his difficulties, is Mrs. Ormonde.

In spite of her endeavours to raise the poor, Mrs. Ormonde still considers them as belonging to another sphere; she has found Thyrza and assisted her, but she does not think her fit to be Walter's wife; she warns him that a marriage such as theirs may result in wretchedness, which will only increase as the years advance. In her heart of hearts she is convinced that Walter will live down his passion; that is the reason why she makes him promise to wait two years; she will take care of Thyrza and never seek to influence her affections.

Egremont has lost all confidence in himself; sincere as he is in his feelings and his utterances, and honest to himself, he can say that he has never spoken of love to Thyrza, but he adds to himself, that still he is not totally without blame, for his silence and his looks have betrayed what he felt; it is all a failure; he has failed in his attempt to reach the artisans, he has failed in his friendship for Grail; how can he believe in his own judgment now? Better be guided by Mrs. Ormonde; it is so much easier than to fight circumstances, and to rouse himself to action; he promises at length to go away for two years.

Full of good intentions to do her duty by Thyrza, Mrs.

Ormonde takes her education in hand; her aim is to make Thyrza independent and for a time she meets with uncommon success; the girl is working with an astonishing cheerfulness; two years — it seems an endless time to Thyrza, but the knowledge that Egremont loves her, a knowledge that has come to her, because she has overheard the conversation that has decided their fate, fills her with a strength that overcomes all difficulties, if only she can become more worthy of him. Egremont has gone to America, where in a manufacturing town in Pennsylvania he is to superintend the works that his firm has just opened there.

It is a life full of action, which leaves him little time for reading and thinking about his private affairs; he does not idealize any longer, but looks at life with clearer eyes than before. Having failed himself, he is able to understand the difficulties of others and wonderful as it seems to him, he can sympathize with men, upon whom he looked down before, considering them beneath his notice. Life has made him humble, and he sees now that his so-called study of modern life was the merest dilettantism, mere conceit, and boyish pedantry. He no longer believes that he has been chosen to reform the world; he has given up all theorizing, and his only endeavour is to become a sound and mature man. In this Walt Whitman is to help him. "He makes one ashamed to groan at anything. Whatever comes to us is in the order of things and the sound man accepts it as his lot. Noble grief there is in him and noble melancholy can come upon him but acquiescence is his last word" [1].

Acquiescence, that has become Egremont's attitude of life; he looks back upon his own past and sees that his philanthropic enterprise has come to an end for good and all, that the future will be the one task to make a woman happy.

[1] *Thyrza*, Ch. XXXV, p. 425.

Still, even his feeling for Thyrza has lost something of its freshness, and the question that puzzles him is, how it is possible that she can go on with her studies in the contented way that Mrs. Ormonde writes about; could she have absolutely forgotten him?

On his return to England he does not speak to Mrs. Ormonde about his love for Thyrza, but about his obligation of marrying her and developing her mind. Just as two years ago he hesitates and follows Mrs. Ormonde's advice to put off his visit to Thyrza.

The suspense and disappointment make Thyrza realize that all her sacrifices have led to nothing; she wants to make amends for the sorrow that she has caused to others, but death prevents her from undoing the past.

Her death is a great shock to Egremont; through life he will be conscious that he has missed something, but that knowledge is in a way an inspiration to him and makes him anxious not lo lose a chance in the years that are coming, not with his old enthusiasm, but sure that the only manner to attain some good is, to give up theorizing and to seize every opportunity of helping those less fortunate than himself. Annabel Newthorpe is willing now to help him and he knows that together with her he will be able to bring a little more happiness into the world.

Thyrza is a story of failure, of a man giving up striving after a solution of the social problem, but again, just as in *Demos,* it is only partly the circumstances that are to blame; it is above everything a failure owing to character, owing to lack of insight, lack of energy and lack of mental strength in Egremont. Gissing has put before us the question, if a mediator could possibly reconcile the two sections of society and his answer is a negative one.

In most of his novels Gissing works with contrasts. In

Demos for instance he has placed the practical social agitator, Richard Mutimer, who likes to see the valley full of model buildings and smoking chimneys, over against the refined, impulsive Hubert Eldon, whose first work is to restore the valley to its natural beauty and who defends his standpoint saying: "I had rather say that I see no value in human lives in a world from which grass and trees have vanished. — The ruling motive in my life is the love of beautiful things" [1]. In *Thyrza* he puts before us Egremont, the idealist, who, before everything, wants to cultivate men's minds and whose endeavours end in failure, side by side with Dalmaine, the practical politician, who values nothing but his own profit and honour, interested in all that concerns the industrial population of Great Britain, without being interested in any individual except himself, the man with a future and sure of wordly success.

In *The Nether World,* the novel that Gissing wrote two years later (1889) he treats the social problem in a way, somewhat different from that in *Thyrza.* What was wanting in Egremont, was the real knowledge of the poor, the daily contact with the workers, and the understanding of their motives. Now Gissing puts the question: "Would not the best person to reach the workers, be one of their own?"

In the picture that Gissing gives of the nether world he has expressed to the full the hatred of ugliness, the loathing of vulgarity that had been the obsession of his own life. He leads us into the byways of Clerkenwell, where sunshine and free air are forgotten things, where the inscriptions on the house-fronts would make you believe that you were in a region of gold and silver and precious stones, but where families herd together in dear-rented garrets and cellars.

"At noon to-day there was sunlight on the Surrey hills;

[1] *Demos,* Ch. XXVI, p. 311.

the fields and lanes were fragrant with the first breath of spring, and from the shelter of budding copses many a primrose looked tremblingly up to the vision of blue sky. But of these things Clerkenwell takes no count; here it had been a day like any other consisting of so many hours, each representing a fraction of the weekly wage" [1].

What Gissing resents, is the absence of simple pleasure and natural beauty in the lives of the poor; throughout the book he repeats the central thought of his first novel: *Workers in the Dawn,* which comes out clearly in the words of Will Noble, the leader of the workingman's club: "I am convinced there must be a rich class and a poor class. But I am not convinced that, of these rich and poor, the one must be a class of brute beasts, of ignorant, besotted, starving, toilworn creatures, whilst the other must be a class of lords and princes" [2].

At the time when Gissing wrote his first novel (1880) his aversion to democratic leaders and socialist agitators had taken root in him already, but he was still spurred on by the hope of finding a remedy; full of indignation he protested against an easy-going optimism. "Let them maintain that these horrors are a necessary condition of the present moment, if they please, but never that we have it not in our power to alter them!" Though there is in this novel a most depressing sense of failure and frustrated hope, yet there is in the terrible gloom a glimpse of light in the idea: "The poor must help the poor, to get out of the mire" [3]. This thought forms the key-note of *The Nether World.* Gissing points out that philanthropic committees fail in raising the poor, and can do nothing but bring a temporary relief. In

1 *The Nether World,* Ch. II, p. 11.
2 *Workers in the Dawn,* Vol. II, Ch. VIII, p. 205.
3 id., Vol. I, Ch. XI, p. 249.

a sarcastic account of the soup-kitchen [1] he attacks the self-satisfied philanthropists who grumble about the ingratitude of the poor. "Have you still to learn that this nether world has been made by those who belong to the sphere above it?" [2], but bitter and sarcastic as he is at times, still Gissing has given utterance in this novel more than in any other to the thought that is born out of his hatred of ugliness: a sense of deep compassion; and once more he shows how poverty is the degrading factor, injuring men's moral nature, and working an irreparable wrong. And in picturing his little heroine, Jane Snowdon, he seems to cry out to the whole world: "Rescue the young, while it is yet time."

Jane, a pale, thin, wretchedly clad child of thirteen, grows up in the house of her aunt, Mrs. Peckover; the girl, by nature timid and sensitive suffers much from the ill-treatment of her benefactors, who keep her out of charity, as they say, but who in fact exploit and tyrannize her. She knows that she will be reprimanded, whatever she does, but a sense of duty makes her run, till she is out of breath, when she has been sent on an errand. The expression of her face is one of constant dread; there is but one bright spot in her existence and that is the kindness of Sydney Kirkwood, a young artisan; the few words he has spoken to her, are of such a wonderful gentleness that she stores them up in her heart.

She is not of a rebellious nature, but the coarseness and the cruelty with which she is treated, awake in her a sense of injustice and are near to embittering her for life. Fortunately she is rescued by her grandfather, Michael Snowdon, who has returned from Australia in the possession of a fortune that he has destined for great ends. The old man keeps his wealth a secret from every one, even from Jane.

1 *The Nether World*, Ch. XXVIII.

2 id., Ch. XXVIII, p. 252.

He has taken two simply furnished rooms, which in the girl's eyes are grand beyond all imagining. It is all so different from the life that she has lived up to now, that sitting peacefully by the fire, she cannot realize her position; she cannot shake off the past. and at intervals starts as if in fear. It seems that she cannot trust the new-found happiness; it is all too good to be true.

And as life goes on in peace and quiet, her eyes lose something of the expression of a hunted animal, but the years of her youth spent in the nether world, have left an indelible mark on her character. On the one hand there is in her a deep compassion that instigates her to interfere and help to the utmost of her power — on the other hand there is the feeling of apprehension of what is coming, the shrinking fear of brutality and the lack of self-confidence; something is broken in her that cannot be mended, even by the most careful hands. In her grandfather she has found not only a protector, but also a great friend; like herself he knows how urgent the needs are of the nether world, and the gospel of unselfishnes that he preaches, finds a response in Jane's heart:

"If we could only learn to be kind and gentle and forgiving — never mind anything else —. We struggle to get as much as we can for ourselves and care nothing for others — think about it; never let it go out of your mind; perhaps some day it 'll help you in your own life."

Jane cannot understand, how she will ever be able to help others; she is not conscious of the great gift that has been granted to her: to have about her a sphere of peace that brings out the best in the people who come into contact with her; Sidney Kirkwood who often visits her grandfather, is the first to feel in the quiet chamber a sensation of restfulness that is so difficult to find in the nether world, and which enables him to regain his old pleasure in nature and art; Pennyloaf Candy, who is saved from ruin by the wish to see Jane Snowdon — and Scawthorn[1] wo finds again some of his youthful idealism, know how much they owe to their unpretentious friend. Her grandfather, best of all, knows her cheering and strengthening influence and it raises in him the expectation that in her he has found the person to realize his dream of helping the poor.

There are times of doubt, however, when he finds that Jane is subject to fits of hysteria, "preceded and followed by the most painful collapse of that buoyant courage which was her supreme charm and the source of her influence"[2], but these fits occur more and more seldom and Michael Snowdon thinks that the time is ripe to entrust Jane with the great work. For years he has watched her anxiously, thinking: "Suppose I can teach her to look at things in the same way as I do myself, train her to feel that no happiness could be greater than the power to put an end to ever so little of the want and wretchedness about her; — suppose when I die I could have the certainty that all this money was going to be used for the good of the poor by a woman who herself belonged to the poor? — There's plenty of ladies nowadays taking an interest in the miserable, and spending their means unselfishly. What I hoped was to raise up for the poor and the untaught a friend out of their own midst, some one who had gone through all that they suffer, who was accustomed to earn her own living by the work of her hands as they do, who had never thought herself their better, who saw the world as they see it and knew all their wants"[3]. The old man's idealism inspires Sidney Kirkwood with enthusiasm

[1] *The Nether World,* Ch. XXII, p. 193.

[2] id., Ch. XV. p. 136.

[3] id., Ch. XX, p. 177.

and makes him believe that, as Jane's husband, he will be able to work together with her for the good of others. Upon Jane her grandfather's solemn words have an altogether different effect; she understands that something great and hard and high is suddenly required of her and the tremor of bygone days comes back upon her, as she listens, and the old anguish of timidity, but just as in the past a kind word from Sidny Kirkwood could reassure her, so now the idea that he has faith in her, enables her to regain her cheerful courage. If he could love and assist her, the appalling responsibility would become a high privilege — but Sidney seeing a temptation in the trust and the possession of wealth, fails her; once morc the earnest voice of Michael Snowdon puts the ideal before her, which means a life of sacrifice and renunciation; it is then that, like a child she shrinks from the new and disturbing things that are required of her and that she pleads in a choking voice: "Don 't ask it of me! Give it all to some one else! I am not strong enough to make such a sacrifice. Let me be as I was before!" [1] — Now it seems that she has lost all, even her grandfather's sympathy, she cannot call back the years of peaceful happiness; life has a good deal of bitterness in store for her; she tries to undo the effect of her words, and she has the satisfaction of regaining her grandfather's confidence, but the old man's sudden death prevents his making another will; the money falls into the hands of Jane's father who squanders it in speculations. Neither to Jane nor to Kirkwood was it given to realize their dreams of happiness and love, but both are to experience that it is good to be constrained to think of another's sorrow. Their lives seem a failure, but: "Where they abode it was not all dark. Sorrow certainly awaited them, perchance defeat in the humble aims that they had set them-

[1] *The Nether World,* Ch. XXXIII, p. 308.

selves; but at least their lives would remain a protest against those brute forces of society which fill with wreck the abysses of the nether world [1].

Just as in the other novels the failure is owing to lack of moral strength; it is not really a failure of the old man's plan and the problem: "Could not the poor be helped by one out of their midst?" is not solved.

Again the last note is one of acquiescence: "Yet to both was their work given. Unmarked, unencouraged save by their love of uprightness and mercy, they stood by the side of those more hapless, brought some comfort to hearts less courageous than their own."

The Nether World has been said to be Gissing's most characteristic work [2], and indeed it is not difficult to trace in the characters of this novel, most of his prevailing ideas: his hatred of vulgarity in Clem Peckover, the degrading influence of poverty in Scawthorne and in Bob Hewett, his aversion to exciting propaganda in Sidney Kirkwood, his distrust of philanthropy in the ladies of Chapter XXVIII, his belief in the power of simple goodness in Pennyloaf Candy and Jane Snowdon and above all his deep compassion for the dwellers in the dark in Mrs. Hewett, and in Clara. The final words: "Yet to both was their work given", lead up, as it were, to Gissing's best-known book: *New Grub Street* (1891). Judged by itself, this novel can hardly be called a sociological novel, still, there is so much in it that is closely connected with the preceding books, that I cannot help giving it a place here. Gissing puts into the foreground the urgent necessity of doing the work that is in harmony with one's nature, disregarding worldly success, but with his usual honesty, he shows at the same time, how poverty

1 *The Nether World,* Ch. XL, p. 392.

2 Arnold Bennett, *Fame and Fiction.*

drags a man down and kills his higher aspirations. It is not the world of the very poor, into which he introduces us this time, but the world of writers and journalists.

Gissing calls this world the valley of the shadow of books, and he shows us in the fate of Reardon in the tragedy of Biffen, how many of the dwellers in that valley are worse off than the miserables of the nether world, reduced as they are to the utmost want, and suffering more than the very poorest, because they are conscious of their intellectual superiority and are filled with bitterness at the degradation. He gives as a contrast the characters of Edwin Reardon and Jasper Milvain, two writers trying to obtain a place in the hungry region of New Grub Street, working each in his own way, and in harmony with his character. The prevailing ideas in this novel are the demoralizing influence of poverty and the gulf between the rich and the poor, and it is this which closely links it to the sociological novel.

When Amy Yule gets acquainted with Reardon, she knows that he has never written a line meant to attract the vulgar; she admires him for his ambition to gain a glorious reputation and his wish to do the work that is worth doing.

His sincerity is an altogether different quality from the honesty that Jasper Milvain brags of. Reardon looks at life and at himself with honest eyes; he wants to give himself and his work for what they are, regardless of the consequences and the opinion of the world. This is the very point where Reardon and his wife are at variance. Amy always sees herself with the eyes of her little world; it is not the life of poverty in itself that fills her with horror, but the thought that her friends will pity her and look down upon her. In this respect she sympathizes with Jasper Milvain, the rising journalist, whose regular topic of conversation is success. He does not pretend to be a good fellow, though he often asserts that he is not so bad, and he openly confesses that he is a cynic, but that it is not his fault; the world is to blame for that, not he. His honesty is a sort of shamelessness, screening his low motives.

Between the two men Amy is placed with a character full of possibilities, on the one side her love for Edwin, her pride in him and in the merit of his literary work. How often in their early married life it had happened that she had given her husband a thrill of exquisite pleasure by her clever appreciation or criticism! And on the other side the wish to shine, to take up a position in society, to be among the successful ones.

She had married Edwin in the expectation that the merit of his work would undoubtedly secure success, but in this she was bitterly disappointed. Amy had met Reardon for the first time, when he had just come from abroad, and when the appearance of his first work seemed to promise him a splendid career; for a short period he was walking on the sunny side of life, full of faith in his power as a novelist, and with an air of self-confidence, which, as a rule, was sadly wanting. Even in the midst of his glorious happiness, he had awoke one night in the week before his marriage and had seen, as in a nightmare, poverty and failure threatening him. "He knew, what poverty means. The chilling of brain and heart, the unnerving of the hands, the slow gathering about one of fear and shame and impotent wrath, the dread feeling of helplessness, of the world's base indifference. Poverty! Poverty!" [1]

But the moment of fear had passed and he believed that their love would be able to overcome all difficulties; the opinion of Milvain that in Amy Yule there was a great deal of pure intellect, caused him only a minute of displeasure;

[1] *New Grub Street,* Ch. V, p. 58.

there was a warning note in it, but he did not heed it and faced life with a courage that might have secured him success, it it had not been for the insurmountable obstacles in his path. "He was the kind of man who cannot struggle against adverse conditions, but whom prosperity warms to the exercise of his powers" [1].

After the first year of their marriage he is utterly depressed, overcome by the practical difficulties, by the urgent necessity of having to write for money, and by the lack of leisure to think out the situation and the characters; it is not his thoughts now that urge him to write, but the threatening fear of poverty that forces him to fill his pages; there is nothing spontaneous in his writing and he knows it and feels how it undermines his mental organism.

It is not for himself that he fears poverty; he even thinks that the possession of money has brought him out of the track and that the shock of happiness has disturbed the balance of his nature, but, as time goes on, and writing is becoming a torture to him, he feels that the loss of his literary power means to him the loss of Amy's love. If only he could keep that, if only she could believe in him, and encourage him, he might achieve what seems impossible now.

But his sensitive pride makes him hide things, and especially conceal his worries from Amy. When he sees, how she brightens at some cheerful news, he becomes more and more conscious that she must not be dispirited by his despair, but that facts must be disguised from her; it is the end of their perfect confidence; and a sense of loneliness comes over him, together with a sense of shame. He accuses himself of cowardly selfishness, not to have listened to the warning voice in his nightmare. He repeats again and again to himself that he has only himself to blame, and

[1] *New Grub Street,* Ch. V, p. 54.

not Amy, for she believed in him, but he foresaw his lack of sustaining power and perseverance.

He is ashamed of the work he does at Amy's request, the work good enough for the market, the work that is to bring in money for her and the child, and in his loneliness he is aware how he begins to hate the little boy, who takes up all Amy's loving care and who has come between him and her. He feels more and more estranged from Milvain, who discourages him with his practical advice and it embitters him to see, how Amy enjoys Milvain's talk of success. He is jealous of every one who is on friendly terms with Amy, and he, who used to blame himself, now feels wronged, and indulges in a sense of self-pity.

More than ever does he hate his work, when it appears in print and he will not take the chance that Milvain wants to give him, to meet people whose acquaintance, as Milvain expresses it, will be a splendid advertisement. He refuses to present himself as the author of the rubbish he has written; if he is ever to succeed, it must be by the merit of his work and not by an undeserved popularity. In this, as in all things Milvain and he are at odds; Milvain's conviction is that "one's own brain would soon run dry; a clever fellow knows how to use the brains of other people" [1].

Fully conscious of the inferiority of his latest novel, Reardon still cannot hear from others what he knows so well himself; having lost faith in himself, he cannot bear pity. In his growing bitterness he envies all people who are rich. — "If one were rich as those people. They pass so close to us; they see us and we see them, but the distance between is infinity. They don 't belong to the same world as we poor wretches. They see everything in a different light; they have powers which would seem supernatural, if we were suddenly

[1] *New Grub Street,* Ch. XII, p. 148.

endowed with them. Between wealth and poverty is just the difference between the whole man and the maimed" [1].

His mind is full of these thoughts of injustice, hatred and envy, and it becomes more and more impossible for him to struggle against circumstances; the tendency to postpone effort is getting stronger and stronger in him and, when Amy proposes that they shall separate for a time and that he shall go to the seaside to recover, he consents, though knowing that a short holiday will not be any use.

But whatever may have changed in him, his sincerity has not died down, and though he has fallen to the temptation of avoiding difficulties, he is honest to himself and understands that he is undertaking the impossible and only putting off the evil day. He, who was too proud, to be praised for bad work, is not too haughty, to accept a clerkship that will bring in one pound a week.

Amy is not the person to appreciate his sincerity; she refuses to share his poor lodgings; she does not pity him; she despises him that he is not even capable of holding up such position as he had gained; she refuses to follow him, now that he does not support her in keeping up appearances. In his bitterness he reproaches her with hard egoism, and makes himself believe that this is not the same woman that he once worshipped; in his conversations with his friend Biffen, the realist, he blames Amy, but it is only in the hope of hearing another defend her, for, deep down in his heart, he knows that he cannot give up his love.

All the time his jealousy of Milvain is increasing, till at last it causes a breach between them, when Reardon accuses Milvain and blames him for the estrangement that has come between Amy and himself. "Your way of talking has always been to glorify success — it has cost me too

[1] New Grub Street, Ch. XV, p. 179.

much"[1]. Milvain knows that it is true; though he tries to excuse himself by saying that he has never purposely influenced Reardon 's wife, still he is aware that the tone of his conversation has been injurious to Amy, for Milvain consciously advancing on the road that leads to worldly success, has not lost the feeling that the unpractical people that he pretends to despise, are on a higher plan than himself; he knows that Reardon has a nobler nature, he is convinced that in Marian Yule's company he is nearer to the better ideals of life, but his vanity and ambition lead him on; and, according to his sister, it is the wisest course for him, because, as she expresses it: "Jasper's moral nature will never be safe as long as he is exposed to the risks of poverty"[2].

His ambition to occupv a place in society is not restricted to himself; he exerts himself to procure for his sisters a respectable position and in this it is not mere selfishness and pride that are at the bottom of his actions; he knows that their impoverished condition is owing to his liberal expenses and he considers it as an act of reparation to help them on in life.

In the relation in which Milvain stands to his sisters, Gissing has made it quite clear that love of money was not the motive power of Milvain's life, but that he considered money as the only means to take up a place among the intellectual leaders; he hates the idea that Maud is going to marry a man, whose only merit is his wealth, knowing that her future life will be one of luxury, but at the same time one of empty gossip. But he has preached too long the gospel of prosperity and has to suffer the consequences now. Often and often he has told his sisters that "all this is contemptible of course; but we belong to a contemptible society and can 't

1 *New Grub Street,* Ch. XX, p. 240.
2 id. Ch. XX, p. 243.

help ourselves" [1], and he has prided himself on his wisdom and "his scent for the prudent course."

We see Milvain at his worst, when this scent for the prudent course interferes with what little idealism is left in him. He feels attracted to Marian Yule, even at the time when she is poor, and is greatly satisfied, when a legacy that she gets from an uncle, makes it possible for him to speak of marriage; but, when things go wrong, when the money is lost, and Marian's home-life becomes a source of trouble to Milvain, he sees love as an obstacle in his way that has to be removed. Only a rich wife will bring him nearer to success; this thought makes him turn away from Marian at the moment that she needs him most and makes him shake off all sensitiveness as sentimental and unpractical.

In striving for popularity he is not scrupulous in the least: he writes criticisms for different papers in different tones; if the world wants to be deceived, and above all, wants to be flattered, well, "answer a fool, according to his folly; supply a simpleton with the reading he craves, if it will put money in your pocket." [2].

At the time that Milvain has chosen wordly success and suppressed his softer emotions, Reardon in the utmost poverty and loneliness turning away from the outside world, finds a comfort in the beauty of his classics, and forgets the squalor of his surroundings in calling back to his mind a marvellous sunset at Athens. "Poverty can't rob me of those memories. I have lived in an ideal world that was not deceitful, a world which seems to me, when I recall it, beyond the human sphere, bathed in sunlight" [3].

In the eyes of the world he is a complete failure; an

[1] *New Grub Street,* Ch. XX, p. 243.
id., Ch. XXXIII, p. 419.
[3] id., Ch. XXVII, p. 336.

over-sensitive, proud man, ruined by weakness of will and lack of self-confidence; in Gissing's opinion "a fine-feeling personality, wholly unfitted for the rough and tumble of the world's labour-market; a type of character ruined by poverty," a restless seeker for beauty, not finding repose before the end of life, whispering to his friend: "It doesn't matter what happens, she is mine again."

Amy under the shock of the child's death and at the sight of her husband's sufferings, has lived through once more the time of her early love. Then life again urges her to activity and she receives from Milvain a letter, together with his appreciation of Reardon's novels, an appreciation that comes too late for the poor seeker, Amy's interest in Milvain and his career awakes anew and her grateful answer leads to a reviving of their friendship; their ambitions are the same: together they are going to find success.

The tone at the end of *New Grub Street* is the glorification of success; Milvain and Amy in their luxurious home enjoying their good fortune, he the editor of one of the leading periodicals, she a brilliant hostess in society. "Is not the world a glorious place?" "Yes for rich people. How I pity the poor devils!"

And yet we feel in this glorification, that Gissing hints at the shallowness of their characters, in Amy's words about Marian: "She nearly ruined your life," and Jasper's answer: "Yes, you are right, she nearly ruined me. And in more senses than one. Poverty and struggle, under such circumstances, would have made me a destestable creature. As it is, I am not such a bad fellow, Amy" [2].

Could we find a more striking contrast than that between

1 *New Grub Street,* Ch. XXXI, p. 387.

2 id., Ch. XXXVII, p. 469.

Milvain's self-satisfaction and Reardon's humble words: "I am afraid I could do nothing worth doing?"

If George Gissing has never really been one of the poor in their outlook on life, at least he has lived with them and suffered with them; this has enabled him to put the reality of their misery before us, while at the same time his lack of humour has prevented him from finding the relieving touches.

Looking back in the period of life, "led in thoughtful stillness"[1], he sees how much of the sorrow, and barrenness and solitude of his youth was owing to the fact that he was poor. He says that those who say that money cannot buy the things most precious, have never known the lack of it.

Of such Mrs. Humphry Ward is one; she sees life with entirely different eyes; she has never lived with the poor, but has visited them and then returned to her own world. As her daughter, Janet Penrose Trevelyan tells, Mrs. Humphry Ward's way of life at Grosvenor Place was naturally one which involved a good deal of expenditure. Sometimes she would have searchings of the heart over this or even momentary spasms of economy, but the thought that a better understanding between rich and poor was at the time the most that could be reached, reconciled her to her sphere of life.

With great energy she worked for the Passmore Edwards Settlement in Tavistock Place, opened August 1902, where men and women of birth and education devote their lives to the service of their less fortunate fellows. The motto of the Settlement: "Man needs knowledge, not only for the sake of livelihood, but for the sake of life," explains what the main object of the institution is, but Mrs. Humphry Ward

[1] *The Private Papers of Henry Ryecroft,* Spring, Ch. V, p. 11.

expected to gain more than mere knowledge; she was confident that many changes in the conditions of life and labour are coming to pass in the future, but she was convinced "that meanwhile a change in men's feelings towards one another might make this world a better and a happier place"[1].

In many respects, advanced as she was, her work breathes the spirit of Kingsley and Mrs. Gaskell: the hopeful tone, the ardent belief in political changes, the conviction that personal contact between rich and poor will do away with wrath and envy.

Yet in other points she is at one with the writers of the third period, in that she too, does not attempt to find a solution.

As S. L. Gwynn has pointed out, "she makes plain the uncertainty and disquiet which harass many honourable minds with the question: "Why should we have so much, when those about us have so little?" [2]

Though she could not see a solution of the social problem, her life was full of a great yearning for the betterment of the lot of the working-classes [3].

In her sociological novel *Marcella,* and the political sequel, *Sir George Tressady,* she has personified her views in the character of Marcella Boyce, and from the beginning we are struck by a sense of compromise, by the fact that Marcella with her socialistic tendencies and her sympathy with the Venturist Society, is an aristocrat deep down at the bottom of her heart.

Life is not easy for little Marcella, the young rebel with her roving, defiant eyes, who in spite of appearances, can never forget that she is one of the Boyces of Brookshire.

1 *The Life of Mrs. Humphry Ward,* by her daughter, Janet Penrose Trevelyan, p. 190.

2 S. L. Gwynn, *Mrs. Humphry Ward,* Ch. III, p. 52.

3 Cf. A. J. Stuart Walters, *Mrs. Humphry Ward,* Her work and influence.

In the eyes of most of her school-fellows she is a little wild-cat, and only few have a notion of the childish loneliness and helplessness in her heart.

Her fantasy is developing into a sort of dramatic instinct, by which as a child she sees herself as the trusted friend and companion of the Prince of Wales and by which in after-life she sees herself, "as the preacher sitting on her stool beside the poor grate"[1]. Her character is full of contradictions, one half of her is impulsive and passionate, the other half looks on, and puts in finishing touches; she makes the impression of being singularly well able to take care of herself and, on the other hand, she is strongly influenced by her surroundings: in her London life she shares the wrath of Socialist friends against the privileged classes, but, once returned to Mellor Park, the old associations take hold of her, and we see her, "struck by the dignified ancestral sound of the breakfast-bell, with a slight unconscious straightening of her tall form stepping into the Chinese room[2].

In the village church she feels herself in her place, "under the shelter of her forefathers, incorporated and redeemed, as it were, into their guild of honour"[3].

Her socialistic ardour has not forsaken her, but gradually it is taking another form; her dramatic instinct helps her to bring about the compromise; it is true that the water-supply is a disgrace, the condition of the cottages a horror, the life of the labourers one of starvation, but then, all depends upon the owner of Mellor, and, inspired by the glory she has in her position, she is full of confidence that she will carve her path, make her own way and be the queen and arbitress of human lives.

[1] *Marcella*, Book I, Ch. VIII, p. 82.
[2] id., Book I, Ch. III, p. 19.
[3] id., Book I, Ch. III, p. 29.

Theory and practice are sadly at variance in her young life; she wants to teach the poor to stand on their own feet, to rouse them to discontent and revolt, and, at the same time, she wants to arrange their lives for them, and she expects gratitude and the willingness to be led by her.

She excuses her philanthropy with the words: "You can't get the changes for a long, long time. And, meanwhile, people must be clothed and fed and kept alive" [1]; "a little charity greases the wheels," [2] but evidently she enjoys the rôle of Lady Bountiful, and is convinced that all depends upon how it is managed, — in the interest of what ideas; she has formed a scheme for reviving and improving the local industry of straw-plaiting in the village, though she knows that it is economically unsound, and is nothing but a stopgap and a temporary palliative. She wants to play an active part in the lives of the labourers, but with a strange inconsistency she blames all landlords in sweeping generalizations.

Life takes young Marcella in hand, and the effect is a toning-down and humbling one.

Instead of being the mistress of Maxwell Court, and, as the wife of Aldous Raeburn, arranging the lives of the labourers and cottagers in her own manner, she is a hard-working nurse in London, who has to fight her way, no longer supported by the old illusion of acting a prominent part on the stage of life; she finds herself slipping away from Socialism more and more and makes her views clear in saying:

"As I go about among these wage-earners, the emphasis — do what I will — comes to lie less and less on possession, more and more on character" [3].

1 *Marcella,* Book II, Ch. II, p. 144.
2 id., Book II, Ch. IV, p. 163.
3 id. Book III. Ch. VI p. 376.

It is not only her experience which has brought about the change, but also the influence of Edward Hallin, the idealist who would build a state on the purified will of the individual man, and wants to be sure that the beauty and the leisure and the freshness are not lost out of the world [1].

Marcella begins to realize that knowledge, cleverness, and influence are nothing compared to character, based on self-surrender and love.

And the great love that life has in store for her is to become the sustaining power of her future, the love of Aldous Raeburn that she wins back by conquering pride and throwing off all outward show. For at the root of her, there is a deep sincerity, a sincerity so great that it leaves all other qualities in the background.

She acknowledges that what is really wanted, is not her help, but their growth; not a complete overthrow of what has come to us from the past, not an entirely new order, but the old order made sound. She looks forward to a happier and better future, conscious that the real barriers that divide man from man, are not mere wealth and poverty; that what is urgently necessary is: "never to give up the struggle for a nobler human fellowship, the lifelong toil to understand, the passionate effort to bring honour and independence and joy to those who had them not" [2].

In this mood Marcella begins her life as Lady Maxwell: "one of the most famous women of her time, watched, praised, copied, attacked, surrounded" [3].

Edward Hallin's words: "Never resign yourself," have become the living truth of her existence, but we cannot help thinking that it is a queer compromise that she has made of her life.

[1] *Marcella,* Book III. Ch. XI p. 435.
[2] id., Book IV, Ch. VI, p. 556.
[3] *Sir George Tressady,* Ch. XXIII, p. 526.

Her true home, she said, was a small furnished house in the Mile End Road, where she received her fellow-workers and her poorer friends, but, happy as she and her husband felt there, it was not a home for little Hallin; so on Saturday-mornings they would leave town and its troubles behind them, to go to Maxwell Court, and all the morning mother and child would be trailing together over field and wood, and in the afternoon the carriages would drive up and Marcella would receive her distinguished guests. And though she calls the simple house in Mile End Road her true home, there is the other house as well in St. James's Square, where Marcella is the kind hostess in a blaze of diamonds.

The compromise appears very clearly from the fact that her days of rest and leisure are not spent among her poorer friends in the East End, but on the glorious lawns of Maxwell Court, where we see her sitting under the cedars in front of the magnificent Caroline Mansion, and believing all the time that to live with the poor, part of every week, makes her one of them. In spite of the burden of responsibility that weighs her down, she believes in the political changes, in the Factory Bill that she and her husband are working for, as a means of removing crying wrongs and glaring contrasts.

"Everywhere the old workshops were to be bought up, improved, or closed: everywhere factories in which life might be decent, and work more than tolerable, were to be set up; everywhere the prospective shortening of hours and the doing away with the most melancholy of the home-trades was working already like the incoming of a great slowly-surging tide, raising a whole population on its breast to another level of well-being and of hope" [1].

There is a note of hopeful trust in the future in this vision of a great slowly-surging tide, a note which is entirely wanting

[1] *Sir George Tressady*, Ch. XXII, p. 498.

in Gissing's novels. Whereas Gissing again and again emphasizes the thought that the gulf between rich and poor is wider than ever, and that nothing but a complete change is able to better the lives of the poor, Mrs. Humphry Ward believes in political changes, in the old order made sound; and where Gissing points out the failure of philanthropy, Mrs. Humphry Ward urges us to put our hand to the plough, and bring about what little changes are possible, relying on the Future to complete our work.

Chapter IV

William Hale White (Mark Rutherford) 1829–1913

Among the writers of the third period William Hale White occupies a unique place. As A. G. van Kranendonk[1] has already pointed out, Mark Rutherford throws a new light on the social conditions of the nineteenth century. In *The Revolution in Tanner's Lane*[2], published 1887, he gives us a realistic picture of the time of ferment, the growing discontent and the revolutionary tendencies among the people and more especially among the Dissenters in London and Manchester between 1814 and 1821, while in the second part of the book he takes us to Cowfold (= Bedford) in 1840, and puts before our eyes his native place, and Tanner's Lane Chapel seen in the light of loving remembrance, but at the same time described with the pen of scrupulous honesty and unsparing realism.

So we can say that according to the time in which he places his characters, his novel belongs to the period of the Revolutionary Novel; judged by the democratic view of the author it belongs to the time of the Democratic Sociological novel, while in *The Autobiography* and *The Deliverance of Mark Rutherford* as well as in *The Revolution in Tanner's Lane* we are strongly reminded of the gospel of sympathy and renunciation preached by the writers of the second period, especially by George Eliot.

[1] A. G. van Kranendonk, *De Engelsche Litteratuur sinds 1880.*
[2] Chapters I—XVI.

In a lecture a few weeks after W. Hale White's death Mark Rutherford [1] was described as a shy and retiring genius and indeed the sphere of thought we find in *The Autobiography* and its sequel *The Deliverance of Mark Rutherford* is that of a man who blames himself, before he finds fault with others, a man who calls to mind his duties, before he claims his rights, a man whose philosophy of life is based on a Stoic submission to the inevitable.

Looking back upon his life at the age of seventy-eight, he sees himself as a young man of eighteen finding a volume of Wordsworth on the bookshelf in the dining-room, opening it at haphazard and reading the lines:

"Knowing that Nature never did betray
The heart that loved her."

This moment was decisive for his further life; it altered his history [2]. — In *The Autobiography* he says: "Wordsworth unconsciously did for me what every religious reformer has done, — he re-created my Supreme Divinity; substituting a new and living spirit for the old deity, once alive, but gradually hardened into an idol" [3].

And in the days of his religious doubts, a feeling of restfulness and peace came over him, when he looked up to the mystery of the stars, or gazed on the downs in the far-away distance, knowing God dwelt in every cloud-shadow which wandered across the valley. Among the moulding influences of his life was the friendship of Ruskin and Morris; even in the most difficult circumstances he refused to earn money by work that is absolutely false and one of the blessings that he wanted to bring to the very poorest is to

[1] A Lecture delivered before the Dundee Branch of the English Association in June 1913.

[2] Cf. *The Early Life of Mark Rutherford* by Himself, p. 61.

[3] *The Autobiography*, Ch. I, p. 19.

find pleasure in work for its own sake; he did not make an attempt to reform the world, being convinced that it was beyond his power, but he felt the hopelessness of the slavery and was touched to the quick by the sullen subjugation that he saw about him.

Just like Gissing he was struck by the immense gulf separating the rich and the poor. He tells how one evening he went with a friend "to hear a great violin-player, who played such music and so exquisitely, that the limits of life were removed. But we had to walk up the Haymarket home between eleven and twelve o'clock and the violin-playing became the merest trifling" [1].

To him the worst of all was that in the squalid alleys of the great towns the instinct to escape, the desire to decorate existence in some way or other was dead among thousands and thousands, for in spite of the courage with which he faced life he could not but confess to himself that he stood powerless and what was more, that he was convinced that "no known stimulus, nothing ever held up before men, to stir the soul to activity, can do anything in the back streets of great cities so long as they are the cesspools which they are now" [2].

Together with his inability to solve his religious problems, the confession that any amelioration in the existing conditions was beyond him, spread a deep gloom over his life, a gloom, clearly manifested in *The Autobiography of Mark Rutherford.* But just as his religious doubts did not lead to a state of negation, but to the declaration: "I don't know", which did not exclude all hope, so the contemplation of the social problem, which made him acknowledge: "I am unable to bring about a change", though it darkened heaven and

[1] *The Deliverance,* Ch. II, p. 23.
id., Ch. II, p. 27.

earth at times, admitted a slight ray of light, bringing the faint hope "that some force of which we are not now aware, might some day develop itself, which will be able to resist and remove the pressure which sweeps and crushes into a hell, sealed from the upper air, millions of human souls every year in one quarter of the globe alone"[1].

In spite of the failure to do some practical good to the poor in general, he saw that he had not been quite useless, and that he had saved two or three, saved not from poverty, but from despair and self-despising; a salvation great enough to encourage a man to do what little good may lie within reach of his hands. "Blessed are they who heal us of self-despisings" was a lesson that his personal life had taught him. In the time when he was depressed by the sense of his utter worthlessness, his failure in practical life, it was George Eliot[2], whose sypathy encouraged and strenghtened him. And it was not only this he owed to her, but, over and above the willingness to accept life, and to renounce selfish pleasures, there was the gift of finding an interest in the most commonplace people, the gift of being aware "that messages from Him are not to be read through the envelope in which they are enclosed"[3].

In his loneliness and his longing for a perfect friendship this gift came to him as a revelation; he saw that the pathos of life is not only to be found in great persons and out-of-the-way places, but that it may be discerned everywhere about in uninteresting and stiff-looking persons, if once our eyes are opened to it.

And in contrast with Gissing, who emphasizes the degrading influence of suffering, Mark Rutherford makes us see the

[1] *The Deliverance,* Ch. V, pp. 65-66.
[2] *The Autobiography,* Ch. IX, p. 124.
[3] *The Deliverance,* Ch. IX, p. 125.

beneficial power of suffering, softening and humbling what was hard and proud, and granting us an understanding, born out of experience, an understanding leading to helpful activity. Thus in different ways he repeats George Eliot's teaching:

"Sympathy is but a living again through our own past in a new form."

On the one hand we find in Mark Rutherford a submission to the inevitable, relieved by the willingness to realize the joy of the moment, the conviction that the duty of duties is to suppress revolt, and on the other hand the stern realism stating that the gulf has not yet been bridged over, bringing home the truth that for immense masses of people, labour instead of being something in which they can take an interest and even a pride is "the merest slavery, as mechanical as the daily journey of the omnibus horse" [1].

One of these toilers is the hero of *The Revolution in Tanner's Lane,* commonplace enough in the eyes of the world, Zachariah Coleman, "a smallish, thin-faced, lean creature." We find him standing among the crowd with a feeling of disdain for the enthusiasm of the multitude. What does he, a fierce Radical, care about Lewis the Eighteenth? "Turn a man out with his digestion in perfect order, with the spring in the air and in his veins, and he will cheer anything, any Lewis, Lord Liverpool, dog, cat, or rat who may cross his path" [2].

There he is standing, one against many, not carried away by the mood of the hour, but steadfast in his principles and honest in his deeds. He cannot lift his hat or hooray with the multitude, and very soon he is at the mercy of a huge drayman who knocks Zachariah's hat off. A sense of in-

[1] *The Deliverance,* Ch. VIII, p. 106.

[2] *The Revolution in Tanner's Lane,* Ch. I, p. 5.

justice drives him to attack his strong antagonist with all the odds against him, and a blow right in his face is his reward.

Fortunately for him the by-standers instantly take the side of the weaker man and a young Major comes to his aid and accompanies him to his lodgings in Clerkenwell.

They were modest enough, these lodgings, for Zachariah was employed as a compositor in a jobbing office in the city, but they were scrupulously neat and tidy, for Zachariah's wife, to whom he had been married just three months, was a woman of rule and order, strict in her religion, strict in the observance of the Sabbath, strict in the worship of her household-gods.

She had the reputation of being a most sensible woman and Zachariah had known her for a long time and admired her for her neatness and good looks. She was one of those who cannot but follow the beaten track, useful so long as the routine of every-day life is not disturbed, but who sadly fall short in critical moments, losing their balance, when things go wrong, or when they are driven out of the security of their self-satisfaction.

Mrs. Coleman's first impression, on seeing her husband's sad plight, was not anxiety or sympathy, but annoyance that the ordinary household arrangements were upset, and irritation at the thought that Zachariah might be ill for some time and at the consideration what a mess there would be.

It is a scene typical of the way, in which Mark Rutherford puts his characters before us, adding just a few insignificant details, which make them stand out, clear and life-like.

For one moment, flattered by the chivalry of the Major, something seemed to stir in Mrs. Coleman's heart and she put her hand on her husband's shoulder; he brightened immediately, sadly as he was in want of sympathy; it gave him courage, moreover, to ask for some tea. "Tea at that time, the things having been all cleared away and washed up! She did not, however, like openly to object, but she did go so far as to suggest that perhaps cold water would be better, as there might be inflammation. Zachariah, although he was accustomed to give way, begged for tea; and it was made, but not with water boiled there. She would not again put the copper kettle on the fire, as it was just cleaned but she asked to be allowed to use that which belonged to the neighbour downstairs who kept the shop."

Though the injury in itself was not serious, the depression that followed it, left Zachariah in a miserable condition; a day without work left him time to think and to see his married life before him, deprived of all glamour, cold and cheerless and grey. He looked at it with the feelings of a man, out in a chilly, drizzling rain. He did not try to ignore facts; he faced life with his usual honesty and realized that in outward appearances nothing had changed, and that he certainly could not accuse his wife of passing herself off on false pretences, that the mistake was his, but also that it was an irremediable one and he was conscious of the bitter truth that he had missed the great delight of existence.

"He was paralysed, dead in half of his soul, and would have to exist with the other half as well as he could" [2]. No self-pity or despair in this commonplace printer; if there was no joy in life for him, he would strive to dismiss his dreams, and do his best with what lay before him. The creed that hedged in Mrs. Coleman and shut out the loveliness of life, was in him a living faith, upholding and strengthening.

Sitting there alone, while his wife was busy about the house, Zachariah also found what a shock the occurence

[1] *The Revolution in Tanner's Lane*, Ch. I, p. 16.

[2] id., Ch. I, p. 18.

in the street had given to his trust in the people, raising the question: "Are they worth saving?" But at the return of normal conditions his thoughts of hesitation and doubt passed away unperceived and left him unchanged in his belief in Democracy, a feeling as deep-rooted in him as his religious faith. So it happened that he readily assented, when the Major invited him to come to the Club of the Friends of the People. There was a great longing in this uninteresting-looking artisan, a love for everything that lifted him above the commonplace; his heart warmed when reading Byron's *Corsair,* it answered to his inmost self, this scorn of what is mean and base, this courage which dared, this love of freedom, but most of all this reality of passion.

But together with these longings there was a stern sense of duty, of humble acceptance without a murmur. "The vision of Medora will not intensify the shadow over Rosoman Street, Clerkenwell, but will soften it" [1].

For a time Zachariah finds a consolation in interests that lead him out of himself, while his wife experiences a new pleasure in the attentions of Major Maitland; she is excited to a degree, when it is arranged at last that Mr. and Mrs. Coleman shall go to the theatre one evening with the Major. Independents as they are they have declined the invitation for some weeks, but finally they have consented to go, on the excuse that a Shakespeare play which you read at home, cannot be a sinful thing when acted on the stage. Mrs. Coleman is in the best of tempers, and the gaiety of his wife is far from embittering Zachariah; it only intensifies his feeling of guilt; instead of blaming her, he reasons that perhaps he is answerable for her silence and coldness, and even when he comes home to an empty room, without any preparations for a supper left for him, he calls himself a fool, for taking it to heart.

[1] *The Revolution in Tanner's Lane,* Ch. I, p. 26.

Still, in spite of his reasoning, he is but human, and he feels hurt and neglected; — but then there is Shakespeare's art, lifting him out of himself; Othello's rash deed is a warning to him and full of the best intentions he goes home, only to find his wife most irresponsive.

It seems that there is nothing but failure and wretchedness before him in the darkness of his sleepless night, and yet, a few kind words of explanation on his wife's part are sufficient to revive his courage and good-will the following morning and he does all he can, to overcome his natural indisposition to talk.

In the Club of the Friends of the People, Zachariah happens to make a new friend for himself, a French shoemaker, called Caillaud, who had come to England nineteen years ago with his little daughter Pauline, a girl of a vivacious temperament and an open nature.

The work-room, at the same time living-room of the Caillauds, is the very contrast of Zachariah's lodgings; not that it is dirty, but things are lying about in an untidy confusion. And yet, in spite of all that it lacks, it fills Zachariah with a sense of comfort and freedom that he has never experienced in his own, neat home. Father as well as daughter are a revelation to Zachariah, not so much in their revolutionary tendencies, as in their outspoken denunciation of religion; he is puzzled and a little out of his element, and still he feels drawn to them by an inexplicable sympathy. Pauline is certainly not the least rebellious of the two; she is bitter in her criticism and hates a procession, whenever she sees one and is "squeezed and trampled on, just because those fine people may ride by"[1].

There is a temptation for Zachariah in it all, not the longing to join them, but the temptation to be silent, to forget

[1] Cf. *The Revolution in Tanner's Lane,* Ch. V, p. 70.

that it is his duty to testify the truth; with a secret pleasure he sees Pauline dance in her own graceful way, filling the poor work-room with beauty and elegance, but almost at the same moment he is ashamed of himself, and can only silence the reproaching voice of his old self with the meagre excuse that she never performs in public. In the time that follows, his mind is filled with a vague uneasiness and when his wife proposes to invite the Major with a view of converting him, he but too readily consents, as it will give him a chance of making up for sinful thoughts, but he makes the condition that Caillaud and his daughter shall be asked as well. When the company are together at tea, Zachariah gets an opportunity to declare his trust in the Supreme Being, and, carried away by his pious fervour, he impresses his visitors, who are awed by the reality of his faith and the deep earnestness of his voice; his wife on the other hand, becomes fidgety, feeling uneasy at the disturbance of of polite conversation and very soon finds a chance of cutting him short by a remark about tea. More and more he feels estranged from her, and at times he is attacked by a great despondency. "Could anybody be better for not being loved? Why had God so decreed?" And not only in his private life do doubts assail him; in his trust in the people too, he is shaken; poor Zachariah has believed in the people implicitly, but he does not know what the masses really are; and now that he comes into personal contact with them, he finds it a bitter disappointment to acknowledge that the men whom they want to help, do not themselves wish to be helped; that even the Friends of the People themselves are not all reliable, let alone noble-minded men, so that it is often necessary that important affairs should be discussed by a few of them.

Tempted by government spies, the Secretary of the Club

betrays their secrets and Zachariah finds himself at Manchester without any means of existence; he hopes against hope to find a support in his wife now; but he meets with nothing but grumbling and childish complaints, and he is fully aware that he has to bow to the inevitable and to face life alone. Wandering through the streets with only one aim, to get work, hungry in body and soul, his burden seems too heavy to bear, but "a man who is strong and survives, can hardly pace the pavements of a city for days searching for employment, his pockets every day becoming lighter, without feeling in after life that he is richer by something which all the universities in the world could not have given him"[1]. His own experience makes him not merely understand, but feel the bitter revolt in the hearts of those who are treated with disdain, simply because they are poor, and ask for leave to work.

Oh, the great relief of meeting a comrade, who will get him a job; how his heart warms and rejoices that his trust in God is being justified! Impulsive as he is, he proposes to his wife to kneel down at once and thank God, but she thinks it more proper, first to take off her things, then he can think over in the meantime, what he is going to say

Life seems to brighten a little for Zachariah, when his friends come to Manchester and the sympathy of Caillaud and Pauline makes things more bearable, but their enthusiastic plans come to nothing; it is the ignorance of the people that stands in their way, the wildness and the lack of organization.

"The governing classes are apt to mistake the absurdity of the manner in which a popular demand expresses itself for absurdity of the demand itself; but in truth the absurd-

[1] *The Revolution in Tanner's Lane,* Ch. IX, p. 133.

ity of the expression makes the demand more noteworthy and terrible" [1].

And again and again, seeing how unwilling the people are to exert themselves for their own benefit, the old, familiar doubt recurs to Zachariah: "Is it worth all the trouble to save them?" but then the enthusiasm of Pauline stirs him and revives his belief in the good cause in a happier state, even if it should be in a remote future, but above all it brings home to him the truth that he has attempted what was too big for him, and that a man should be content, if he cannot save a man, "to struggle and die to save a little bit of him — to prevent one habit from descending to his children" [2]. Zachariah's sufferings have only just begun; he has to fly to Liverpool, leaving his wife dangerously ill behind. After some days of the utmost poverty and wretchedness he is taken up in the Workhouse Infirmary, but again the effect of his bitter, personal sufferings is not a hardening one.

He is touched to see, how the poor help the poor without any ostentation. "What are we made for, if not to help one another?" [3] Lying idle, his brain is constantly busy, planning out the future, wanting to make his married life more harmonious by his own will-power. But once more Zachariah is to find that outside the pale of everyday happenings he does not meet with any response, that he cannot think his wife's thoughts, but has to follow where his best feelings call him. He goes to see Caillaud in prison a few days before the French enthusiast is to be hanged as a dangerous rebel, knowing that his visit there exposes him to great risks, but not minding personal discomfort, when his friend wants him. The result is that he has to live in prison himself for two years.

[1] *The Revolution in Tanner's Lane,* Ch. XI, p. 159.
[2] id., Ch. XI, p. 163.
[3] id., Ch. XIV, p. 209.

In the second part of the book Zachariah has retreated into the background; we meet him again as an old man, leading a peaceful life with his granddaughter Pauline; a man who, in spite of bitter experiences has remained faithful to his old beliefs, and yet has learned a great truth, disappointing to youthful enthusiasts, the truth that life was not: "yes or no", but that it had become: "yes and no"; not a chasing of dreams, but an acceptance of realities.

Acceptance of realities is the keynote of W. Hale White's teaching everywhere; still we must bear in mind that his gospel of submission to the inevitable is a humble bowing to the Supreme Will, and by no means excludes a sense of personal responsibility.

Not a shallow optimism jubilant in the changes for the better it has brought about and making believe that it is to put an end to all grievances in a near future, but the honest confession that our achievement is ridiculously small, a confession which should lead to the determined resolution to go on, however slight the progress may be; this is the preaching of W. Hale White, "to the end a seeker, and in no mean degree a finder" [1].

[1] Sir W. Robertson Nicoll, *Memories of Mark Ruthferford,* Ch. V. (1924).

Chapter V

Arthur Morrison 1863, Richard Whiteing 1840

The two writers, whose sociological novels bring us to the end of the 19th century, Arthur Morrison and Richard Whiteing put before us the two worlds, that of the rich and that of the poor, so sharply outlined in the West End and the East End of London, and make us realize that the gulf between them is wider than ever. They lay the problem before us, without trying even to hint at a solution; they only probe the wound, stirring our pity, emphasizing the thought that the luxury and wealth of the few can only be had at the expense of the misery of the many and rousing us with the cry: "Save the young!"

Arthur Morrison was born in Kent on the 1st of November 1863 and spent the first ten years of his manhood as a clerk in the civil service. But the mechanical work that he had to do, did not satisfy him and, in 1890 he took to journalism. After his *Tales of Mean Streets* (1894) he designed a novel: *To London Town,* which however, did not appear before 1899. In this he gives a realistic picture of town-life, as it is seen by the eyes of Johnny, who has spent his youth in a tiny cottage near Epping Forest, a life of comparative poverty, but of simple joys. The characters are given in outline rather than in elaborate details, but what strikes us from the beginning is, on the one side the grim earnestness with which Arthur Morrison draws the situation, on the other side a sense of humour, so rare in the sociological novel, which enables him to give us a glimpse of the real outlook of the poor themselves. The picture of contrasts showing London Town and the country near Epping Forest is not drawn in mere black and white, assigning all the sunshine to the country and all the gloom to London, though indeed the London Johnny first learnt to know in Harbour Lane was not a welcoming one. After his grandfather's death Johnny's mother was forced to sell the little cottage and to leave the country, not seeing a chance of earning enough by the butterfly-trade; it seemed that the atmosphere of London, coming nearer and nearer was driving the butterflies away.

It is a sad breaking with the past and a hard beginning in the little shop in Harbour Lane. But life is not all depression in London Town. Soon they find out that there is a comfort in living among their fellows. "For the token and sign of friendship in Harbour Lane was the loan or the exchange of paint. It was the proper method of breaking the ice between new acquaintances and was recognized as such by general sanction. The greeting: "Bit of blue paint any use to ye?" and the offer of the pot across the back fence, were the Harbour Lane equivalents of a call and cards, and the newcomer made early haste with an offer of yellow or green paint in return. It was a permament condition of life in Harbour Lane and thereabouts, that everybody owed everybody else some amount of Paint, and was owed Paint, in his turn by others. So that a complicated system of exchange prevailed, in which verbal bills and cheques were drawn" [1].

Like Gissing, Morrison considers, what is usually called philanthropy as useless West-Endism, virtuously conscious of doing its duty toward the Submerged. Johnny's first acquaintance with the dwellers in the West End was at the

[1] Arthur Morrison, *To London Town,* Ch. IX, p. 85.

Institute, where he attended the drawing-class. "There were sometimes superior visitors from other parts, oozing with inexpensive patronage, who spoke of Johnny and his companions as the Degraded Classes, who were to be Raised from the Depths."[1]

But Morrison differs from Gissing, in as far as he points out the never-failing power of personal contact and sympathetic understanding. This we see embodied in Father Sturt in *"A Child of the Jago"* (1896). We can safely say that Father Sturt stands for Arthur Osborne Jay, Vicar of Holy Trinity, Shoreditch, a man who certainly is not one of "the foolish prophets, that follow their own spirit, and have seen nothing"[2]. It is with the motto: "Woe unto the foolish prophets," that Arthur Morrison heads his story of the Jago, a square of two hundred and fifty yards off Shoreditch High Street, where the human population swarmed in thousands. Just as in *To London Town* Arthur Morrison shows up in *A Child of the Jago* the false optimism of the West-Enders, whose experience about the East End is limited to the neat clerks, the smart young artisans and the tradesmen's sons who occasionally pass their evenings at the East End Elevation Mission and Pansophical Institute, three quarters of a mile east of the Jago's outermost limit.

The aim of the Institute is the Enlargement of the Understanding and the Embellishment of the Intellect. Full of bitter sarcasm Morrison speaks of the subscribers who, on visiting the Institute are astonished at the wonderful effect they have reached and the immense improvement of the Degraded Classes, the Uninformed and the Submerged, as they call them; he has a smile for the self-satisfied authority of the young missionaries who report on their return to the West

[1] Arthur Morrison, *To London Town*, Ch. XXIII, p. 222.
[2] Ezekiel XIII:3.

End that the East End is nothing like what it is said to be [1].

Arthur Morrison takes us to the blackest hole of the blackest pit in East London, called Jago Court, and shows us the outlook of the poorest of the poor; he draws his picture with a realism born out of true insight and sympathetic understanding, introducing us to a world with a law and a morality of its own, this Jago world, apparently so totally different from ours, in reality inhabited by human beings who in spite of their depravity, have a fund of human tenderness, and helpful kindness, a sense of solidarity and brotherhood, which are sometimes sadly wanting among their more favoured fellow-beings.

But at the same time he points out that these finer feelings are doomed to die in the grip of the Jago, and he makes us realize the sad waste of humanity in the character of Dicky Perrott. When we first make his acquaintance Dicky is a small boy who looks like a child of five, but is in reality eight or nine years old; he has a pair of sharp eyes in his pinched, serious face, and he gathers a secret knowledge of all that happens about him in the Jago.

Young as he is, he gets initiated in the law of solidarity by old Beveridge, the veteran of the Jago, who teaches him that it will never do to see too much, and that the worst crime is to betray a Jago, even if he should be your greatest enemy. The supreme commandment is: "Thou shalt not nark!" Dicky has never spoken at home about his store of knowledge, but when his mother gives him the advice, always to be respectable and straight, he cannot bear being treated like a kid and he attacks her with a series of questions: "Where did the yellow necktie-pin come from that father brought home? Where did the money come from to

[1] Cf. Arthur Morrison, *A Child of the Jago,* Ch. II.

pay the rent?" and he does not heed her rebukes, but announces his great plans for the future.

It is his ambition to be in the High Mob, i. e. to steal wholesale. And he is not to be frightened by the fear of prison; only the stupid ones are caught. "I ain't a kid. I know."

Indeed it is no use hiding things from Dicky in this world of crime and squalor; he knows the loose floor-board right of the hearth that is lifted when father comes home with his booty, and in his heart he is proud of his father who is strong in fighting and clever in stealing. Shamming sleep, he lies crosswise at the extreme end of the untidy bed, his mind wide awake, hoping father has done a good click, because that might mean bullock's liver for dinner.

Though he does not feel a kid any longer, he often stands with his little nose pressed against the window of the cake-shop in High Street, especially on days when at home there is not much more than a crust to be had, but at the Opening Ceremony of the new wing of the Pansophical Institute there is a better chance; he is full of a desperate design: to get in and find the cake which he knows will be there in abundance after the ceremony is over.

His endeavours are crowned with unexpected success; he not only snatches at the cakes, but runs home, full of pride in his first click, the Bishop's watch in his little fist.

The glory of being a man and an honour to the Jago and the bitter sense of injustice, when he is mercilessly beaten by his father!

It is not so much the punishment that hurts, but the lack of sympathy in his success; there is not a human soul in whom he can confide — but, there is always as a last resort Jerry Gullen's canary, not a bird, but the old donkey in the back-yard that often harrows the neighbourhood with his bray.

There is a sort of solace in the welcome of his shaggy friend, the twitching of the donkey's ears, and Dicky, grown-up as he feels is sobbing out his sorrow, with his arms about the mangy neck. "O, Canary, it is a blasted shame!"

Dicky's father does not belong to either of the rival families in the Jago—like the Montagues and the Capulets in Verona, so the Ranns and the Learys lived in never-ending enmity — but Dicky has found a comrade in ambitious adventure in Tommy Rann; to him he can boast of his first glorious feat, when the worst of grief has passed over, but his vain-glory is to cost him dear.

Mr. Weech, the owner of a coffee-shop has an eye for the chances there are in the little rat of the Jago. On hearing Tommy Rann's version of the wrong that Dicky has suffered at home, he makes up his mind to catch the boy for his own purposes; Mr. Weech's philosophy being, that the best way to rise in the world and get most of the profits is doing no wrong and believing no wrong, but benevolently buying the things that the Jagos have "found". Dicky falls an easy prey to the temptation of food, and the extreme kindness of Mr. Weech.

"And indeed, from some queer cause, he felt an odd impulse to cry. It was the first time that he had ever been given anything, kindley and ungrudgingly" [1]. But with the worldly wisdom of his nine years he readily understands that he will have to pay in one way or other. In Dicky Perrott's world people do not give things away; that would be the act of a fool.

He feels himself morally obliged to "find" something for his benefactor, who inspires him with a mysterious awe; Mr. Weech seems to know everything and then — he has called him a sharp boy who can find things every day;

[1] *A Child of the Jago.* Ch. VI, p. 59.

he must take his share; if he does not find them, another will, and he has just as much right as the others.

He sees the future before him as the land of promise: always enough to eat, and money to buy a little cart to wheel Looey in, and a boat from the toy-shop with sails, for himself! All that is tender and chivalrous in Dicky stirs him up to action at the thought of Looey, the neglected baby at home, like himself nothing but a nuisance to mother, who is gradually falling into the Jago ways, and giving up the fight for responsibility; Looey, his little sister, who was crying so piteously after the fight in the street, when mother was attacked by the Learys, because of her superior airs.

Superior airs! they had better look out for that Roper family in the neighbouring room, everything tidy and in its place, even a strip of carpet on the floor! There would be boy, Dicky's chance.

In crossing the landing he is attracted by a clock on the mantelpiece of the Ropers; it is not gold, but it can go, it is going! One second he stands — then he darts into the room and disappears with the clock under his jacket. Halfway the stairs he is stopped by his enemy, the hunchbacked Roper but what does he care for him?

What a treasure to have a clock of your own! Oh, if he could show the inside to Looey — but that cannot be; he must take it to Mr. Weech, hard as it is to part with it. And then, full of grief at the loss, all at once the thought flashes upon him, how the pale woman must miss her clock, and for the first time he is assailed by doubts as to the Jago views.

It is the very day when he is confronted with the Rev. Sturt, a being from that other world, but who moves about the Jago as one of them, with an unflinching confidence, which is to become his greatest power.

Dicky is mystified by this stranger with his authoritative

bearing, who fearlessly stands up for the Roper family and carries his point. Nobody knows about the clock, but still Dicky feels that something is wrong; he cannot get rid of that worrying thought and he knows that he must make amends. Another click for the Ropers — that's the way.

Roaming about the streets he has an easy chance of snatching a music-box out of a little girl's hands, but then, she has only one — and the shopkeeper has more than he can play. It only means more trouble for himself, to risk the danger of being caught by the owner of the shop, but he does not mind that.

The music-box is a thing of greater value than the clock in Dicky's eyes, because of the melody that is in it; standing alone in the back-yard and turning the handle, the little boy's lips part, his eyes seeking illimitable space; he plays the tune through, and plays it again. Better not look at it again, for it only makes it harder to part with it and part with it he must! And when at last he has hidden the box among the goods of the Roper family, ready for removal, he vainly tries to persuade himself that he is not sorry.

His doubts about the Jago views disturb his peace of mind, getting into conflict with his ambition to be one of the High Mob, but the sight of some real Toffs is rather convincing, one in furs, another in a fine tall hat, as Old Beveridge points them out to Dicky, directing his pipe to the window of the taproom. Dicky but half understands what the old man means, but the words stick in his memory: "That's your aim in life. It's the best the world has for you, for the Jago's got you, and that's the only way out, except gaol and the gallows. So do your devilmost!" [1]

There is great excitement in the Jago life, it is true; Dicky enjoys nothing so much as seeing a good fight — his father

[1] *A Child of the Jago,* Ch. XI, p. 112.

taking revenge for the attack on his wife is a sight worth witnessing, Dicky screaming from the window of their room: "Good luck father, go it, father!" And on the evening of that same day the rumour goes that the Perrotts are in double luck, for not only has Josh won the fight, but by the death of little Looey they are sure to get the insurance money; at the time that father and mother consider Mother Gap's taproom the best place to rejoice in Josh's success and forget their trouble, "in the darkening room an inconsiderable little corpse lay on a bed, while a small ragamuffin spread upon it with outstretched arms, exhausted with sobbing, a soak of muddy tears: "O Looey, Looey; can 't you' ear? Won 't you never come to me no more?" [1]

Through the influence of Father Sturt, Dicky is sent to school, where he is classed as a half-timer; he cannot spare the time for regular attendance, for he a is notable success as a scout for young vagabonds.

There is nobody to find fault with him now; father takes no heed of what Dicky is doing, and mother never speaks about respectability any more, having accepted destiny; there is only one thing to worry him, and that is the clock of the Ropers on the mantelpiece at home; father has brought it one day from Mr. Weech's in exchange for some stolen goods; and the sight of it is no longer a pride and a joy, neither does it fill him with repentance, but it reminds him of the hunchback, who has come into his life again at school, — a tell-tale who is at the back of every ill chance; not only that he has betrayed him more than once to the teachers, but he also invents stories and incites the bigger boys to fight Dicky, till at last the feeling of hatred grows upon him to such a degree that he does not wait for specific provocation, when he can take revenge on the hunchback.

[1] *A Child of the Jago,* Ch. XIII, p. 142.

In spite of his irregular attendance Dicky picks up some sort of knowledge of reading and writing and Father Sturt finds him willing to lend an ear, when suggesting that Dicky is capable of something better than other Jago boys. Of course Father Sturt is ready to help him, and Dicky knows how much that help is wanted, for the Jago address is a topsy-turvy testimonial for miles round.

Mother is induced to mend his clothes; nobody can disobey Father Sturt and Dicky is installed as a shopboy in Mr. Grinder's business; he has never felt so happy and good before, watching the saucepans, lamps and mousetraps outside the shop, learning the prices, and anxious to serve the customers. "In his day-dreams he saw himself a tradesman, with a shop of his own and the name R. Perrott with a gold flourish over the door. Truly Father Sturt was right: the hooks were fools, and the straight game was the better" [1].

Every new duty is a fresh delight; in his business-like appearance he longs for some Jago friend to pass and view him in his new greatness. He refuses to secrete treacle in a mug for Tommy Rann and full of dignity ignores his enemy, the hunchback. And though his enthusiasm for work as an amusement cools down in a day or two, his pride in it remains.

Alas — the Jago had got him — Mr. Weech misses Dicky's custom and over and above that he is afraid the boy in his new station might tell a secret or two. On the sly he visits Mr. Grinder, kindly advising him to get rid of the new shop-boy as soon as possible. Again Dicky is confronted with the mysterious ways of the world; coming back to the shop with his beloved trolley, and filled with a sense of responsibility, because he carries his master's money, he is sent away without any explanation; he is all incomprehension, and he

[1] *A Child of the Jago.* Ch. XVIII, p. 191.

feels the sobs coming, but he turns at the door and says with tremulous lips: "Won't you give me a chance, Sir, I have done my best." It is all in vain, the whole world is against him; it must be a defect of nature which he cannot understand — was it a sick feeling like this that made little Neddy Wright put an end to his life?

"Dicky was thirteen, and at that age the children of the Jago were past childish tears; but tears he could not smother, even till he might find a hiding-place; they burst out shamefully in the open street. — Who was he, Dicky Perrott, that he should break away from the Jago and strain after another nature?" [1]

But he is not going to give way to bitter despair, he is no longer a child, if he is of the Jago, well then he will do his devilmost and with a brave heart he will accomplish his destiny, a Jago rat, but Father Sturt he must avoid; he had rather fifty beltings than Father Sturt's reproaches.

It is certainly a great disappointment to Father Sturt, but the boy's keeping away pleads against him, and this disappointment is one of many hundreds.

Meanwhile Dicky is puzzled by the thought, who can have informed Mr. Grinder, and it is the clock on the mantelpiece that helps him out of the difficulty; of course his old enemy is at the back of it all again.

Luck seems to have deserted the Perrott family; his father is caught by the police in an unaccountable way, just when at the appointed time he is going to take a watch to Mr. Weech's. It seems very mysterious, till Josh sees Mr. Weech peep from behind a curtain, as he passes, and he instantly knows who has betrayed him, but he is going to keep his revenge to himself, when he comes out again — he can wait.

In the coming years it is hard for Dicky to find food for

[1] *A Child of the Jago,* Ch. XXI.

mother and the baby; besides he has to be careful; the responsibility of having a family to keep, weighs upon him and he cannot risk being caught — what would happen to mother and little Em, if he should be sent to a reformatory.

He grows up lanker and weaker because of the scarcity of meals, and yet he is no longer an easy prey to Mr. Weech's offer of food — he wants money and he has become cautious; he suspects that there is a reason for Mr. Weech's politeness and generosity, just on the day when his father is coming out.

The day is one of feasting and rejoicing, but the state in which Josh finds his wife and children fans his revenge to a mad fury, and he has but one aim: to kill the informer. Regardless of the consequences he follows his brute instinct.

There is no escape for the murderer; in the years that he spent "in the country", the protecting Jago Court has been pulled down and Josh knows that the end is there — well, he will face it as a man.

Courage till the end — that's the thought that also haunts Dicky, as he is sitting with mother behind the glass partition that rises at the side of the dock. But when the end has come, there is nothing but a numb, embittered fury in him. What should he do now? His devilmost! He, a Jago with a hanged father; it would be a comfortable thing to die, but he cannot leave mother and the children; "If only they could go off easily together and wake in some pleasant place like Father Sturt's sitting-room — but, what foolishness! The Jago held him fast — Father Sturt was the only good man — as for the rest, he would spoil them when he could" [1].

In this mood it is a relief to hear about a good fight, a greater relief still in doing something violent.

[1] *A Child of the Jago,* Ch. XXXVI, pp. 340-341.

Dicky is heart and soul in the contest, when all at once he feels a punch under the arm from behind and rolls face under, just catching a glimpse of the hunchback running for his life.

Fate has decided for the Jago rat — he is carried to the surgery on a shutter — it is a question of minutes. Father Sturt bends over him and takes his hand.

"My poor Dicky, who did this?"

"Dunno, Fa'er," The lie — the staunch Jago lie. Thou shalt not nark!

"Tell Mist'Beveridge there's 'nother way out—better" [1].

Dicky's life and death, as Arthur Morrison draws them in his simple way are an earnest and pathetic appeal to save the young; for, though the story is certainly a loud protest against unfruitful optimism it is not the utterance of unrelieved pessimism. In the person of Father Sturt, Morrison shows his belief in personal influence in the social question, the personal influence of a man who goes his way, doing his duty unshrinkingly, not caring about the opinion of the world; even Father Sturt had enemies among the Sentimental Cocksure who condemned him as a man of vulgar and brutal tastes; he did not mind them; it was enough for him to do his every-day duty, to go on sowing the seed, grateful for having kept a few from ill-behaviour, though conscious that the burden was growing day by day. "The thing 's hopeless perhaps," he used to say, "but that is not for me to discuss. I have my duty" [2].

When we compare Arthur Morrison and Richard Whiteing, it seems at first sight, as if this personal note is entirely wanting in Whiteing, and moreover it strikes us that the psychological element comes far less to the fore in *No. 5.*

[1] *A Child of the Jago,* Ch. XXXVII, p. 344.
[2] id., Ch. XXVIII, p. 274.

John Street than in *A Child of the Jago,* but on closer examination we shall find that the note of personal influence is there all the same, though it should be sought in other relations; it is not the uplifting power of one, superior in insight and education, bringing out the best in those below him; it is the strengthening and cheering influence of one of the workers themselves; a girl, lacking in education, but sustained by an upholding and protecting power. It is the ideal of Jane's grandfather [1] come true.

Whiteing, it is true, does not analyse his characters in detail, he works them out by way of contrast, just as he has based the whole plan of his novel on contrasts. The thought of working in this way came to Richard Whiteing in the period of life, when he first took to journalism. As a boy at college he had been a conservative of conservatives; in his autobiography. *My Harvest* [2], he remembers the night when with the other juniors he was squatting on his bed in one of the dormitories and discussing the Chartist Rising of 1848 with his school-fellows, and how disappointed they were that nothing had happened, and how unanimous they were in their opinion that the rabble ought to be massacred to a man. He remembers how later when he had become apprenticed to Benjamin Wyon, an engraver, the truth had come home to him that he had missed much in his one-sided bringing-up, how he began to read voraciously, and joined the Working Men's College in Great Ormond Street, and became conscious that this was the beginning of his real education.

Taught by the pick and pride of England, Maurice, Kingsley, Ludlow, and Furnivall, the great Shakespearian scholar, he was permeated by their ideals, and striving, not in the first

[1] Cf. G. Gissing, *The Nether World,* Ch. XX.
[2] Richard Whiteing, *My Harvest,* (1915).

place "to better his position, but to better his mind as the organ of his soul and to get access to the best thought of all the ages as a means to that end"; aiming, not at an overthrowing and pulling down, but at a patient building up by plain speaking, simple living, and the hatred of all pretence.

Still Richard Whiteing did not feel quite at home in this sphere — there was something in the practical side of the problem that appealed to him, and in 1866, he went to Paris to invite the French workmen to co-operate with their English brethren in showing what they could achieve on their own account without the assistance of the capitalist; the idea was not entirely his own; it was started by his associate at Benjamin Wyon's.

Seeing his own life spread out before him, he is aware, how much he owes to this friend, who suggested to him that, if he is to be successful in his writing, he ought to write about the thing nearest to his heart, he with his "everlasting sense of contrasts between high and low, wise and simple, rich and poor" [1].

This suggestion led to Whiteing's article in the Evening News: *A Night in Belgrave Square by a Costermonger.* It was the first of a whole series, called the Costermonger Articles, and it brought about a complete change in his life. He had found himself and had come to the knowledge that he was to be a writer for the rest of his days; moreover, he felt that his note was to be "plain speaking, simple living and the hatred of all pretence", even though it should be in a more democratic sense than that of his teachers. After his work at Paris, a mission to Russia, and two visits to America, he came back to London and saw life, as it were, with new eyes. He found that the majority of the good Victorians were still inclined to report "no change",

[1] *My Harvest,* Ch. XVIII. p. 255.

though some pessimists were not so cocksure and self-satisfied. He himself, a fighter for the Democratic Cause, still saw that the old ways were very good ways, with due adaptation to the needs of the time and with Morris he preached that what is wanted in the first and foremost place is by all means to learn "the job of your workshop, whatever it may be, founding a science, or cooking a beefsteak. But your head and your hands are not enough, the true source and sustainer of all the powers must still be the heart"[1]

It was this thought that induced him to write the remarkable book, *No. 5. John Street;* it is a sequel to a Utopian story, called *The Island* which Whiteing published in 1888, a book written in the spirit of Gulliver's travels. — The author is driven out of England by the haunting thought that human society is out of focus. One summer afternoon standing on the steps of the Royal Exchange, he looks down on the noisy crowd and sees the East End marching West to demonstrate for the right to a day's toil for a day's crust. The sight gives him a sickness in the region of the heart that robs life of all joy; his only hope is that distance may be a remedy; so he leaves England and visits Paris and Geneva, but it is all the same — society out of focus too. Then giving civilization the slip, he lands by accident on a small island of solid rock, a peak in the Pacific; here he is kindly taken up by the chief magistrate, the ruler over a hundred souls, who carries about the few laws of the island in a small pocket-book.

The touching quality of this simple man and his daughter Victoria is their loyalty to the mother-country and their deep-rooted respect for its civilization, of which they know next to nothing, but which in their eyes is the acme of all goodness and nobility and the happy possession of large

[1] *My Harvest,* Ch. XXIII, pp. 331-332.

things to live for. In comparing the simple goodness of the islanders with the so-called civilization of England, the poor seeker realizes with a sense of bitterness, that "the great mark of all progressive nations is that struggle of each man to make some other do his dirty work for him, which is commonly known as aspirations for the higher life" [1], and he feels that Victoria in her simple criticism has gone to the root of the matter, where she says: "All your plans seem to begin by taking something for yourself, everlasting No. 1; "take, take, take", and so your world goes round; I wonder if it would not go round as well to "give, give, give" [2].

And he thinks he has hit upon the remedy, which is as simple as Victoria's philosophy: Accept the rule of the Blessed Isle: "Each for all" instead of the cry at the Royal Exchange: "Each for himself." With this thought he leaves the Islanders, when his mother's illness calls him back to England, resolved to cut away all hindrances and to begin a healthy life.

In *The Island* Richard Whiteing has contrasted the reality of life in England with his dream of a Utopian state in the Blessed Isle; in *No. 5 John Street* he puts over against each other the luxurious life of Mayfair and the poverty-stricken existence of the EastEnd, both realities; still, the Utopian idea is not lost sight of, but serves as a background. He pretends that he has taken it upon him as one of the executors of a rich friend, to represent the little community of the island in the Pacific at the Diamond Jubilee of the Queen; the settlers desire to testify their patriotic joy and to do something in acquittal of their huge debt to Engeland for moral example; his task includes the writing of a Report for the Governor. He feels that, in order to give the Islanders a fair

[1] R. Whiteing, *The Island,* Ch. XIV, p. 129.
[2] id, Ch. XV, p. 148.

view of the civilization of the motherland, he ought to tell them about "the other half" of society as well, and that a conference on the social question at the Mansion House leaves him as ignorant as he was before; that a University settlement at the East End gives no more than a peep-hole, through which he can only catch a glimpse of the life of the East-Enders, and that the only way to get nearer to realities is to go and see himself, and to live as one of them.

What strikes him at the outset is the horrible state of the dirty feeding-shed, where the workmen take their breakfast and he cannot help thinking of another table with spotless damask and flowers; what impresses him is the unloveliness of this life of the poor, destitute of beauty far more than of mere bread and butter; the uncertainty and dread of having but a few paltry shillings between them and absolute destitution. Trooping into the factory after the meal there is no hypocritical pretence of labour as joy. Lack of beauty, dread, absence of joy in work in their life out-of-doors; absence of rest and lack of personal freedom at home. The door of No. 5 John Street is always open, night and day and at all hours the quiet of the four-storied hovel is broken by harsh noises, but worst of all are the spiritual privations, the vulgarity, the bestiality of the Sunday-papers, appealing to the bad taste of the uneducated.

Yet it is not all gloom in the sphere of No. 5. John Street; there is a simplicity in his garret with its monastic style that gives him a sense of freedom, an insight in the truth "that the right way to belong to yourself is to have as few possessions as possible of other kinds" [1]. Then there is the helpfulness he meets with from the fiirst day of his arrival in this new land and the good breeding, with which all personal questions or remarks are put aside; everywhere

R. Whiteing, *No 5 John Street,* New Edition (1902), Ch. III, p. 27.

he comes across a forbearance and a solidarity, such as he has never dreamt of.

It is a world in itself, this No. 5 John Street, inhabited by all sorts and conditions of men, and he is introduced to the intimate life of this world by his fellow-worker, Old Covey, a man who takes life philosophically and finds his beauty in imitating bird-calls, purely for the pleasure of his friends and himself. His peace of mind is only disturbed for the time being by the various visitors in No. 5 John Street, the missionary, the Red Women, the sanitary inspector, the salvationist; all religious, social, legal or moral agencies are but like a storm passing over John Street, like the wind high in the topmost branches of the trees, leaving nothing behind but a sense of regained quiet.

Old Covey introduces him to Azreal, the anarchist, whose meetings in the wooden shed Covey always attends with pleasure, gathering that anarchy is a system, under which everybody is to do as he likes, and those who won 't do it, shall be made; the programme is interesting enough, varied as it is by discourses on the effect of explosive forces.

Forestalling Covey's introduction, he makes the acquaintance of Tilda; the first Saturday night, sitting at his garret-window, with his week's wages in his pocket, contemplating how much he has learned from his stay in this crowded house, as to discipline in truth and the realities, he is startled by a sudden tumult in the back yard, and a shriek of murder.

Rushing down he is struck by the prominent figure in the group of wild creatures in the full moonlight. It is that of a tall, powerful girl, an Amazon, whose fighting instincts have been roused at the sight of a little boy, attacked by a drunken sailor-man. Stirred on by a sense of injustice, she faces the danger with dauntless defiance, but when the fight is over, she gives way to softer emotions, and bursts into tears as she catches the poor kid that seems to belong to nobody, into her arms.

Tilda's is the only room that has flowers on the window-sill, and when he sees her by daylight, framed by the window, it strikes him that she is unquestionably a fine woman, but that "her expression is her strong point, all fire, energy, dare-devil and untamed will" [1]; fighting, when she is mad, but fighting in order to protect the weaker ones, she is an object of adoration to her neighbours in John Street, Nance, an anaemic factory-girl, and Mammy, the old bedmaker, who feel Tilda with her cheering strength as a hold in their hard lives.

At Tilda's tea-party Old Covey fills the room with the clear and tremulous music of the woods; it is thrilling and poetical beyond measure, but it is followed by the touching remembrances of Covey's youth, which call forth a "Poor little kid" from Tilda.

A moment later all her fury flares up at some insulting cries from the yard; the devil of the back streets is in her defiant port, a noble savage, this coster girl!

Covey makes him acquainted with the ups and downs in No. 5 John Street, and shows him that even in this sober life there are compensations, as long as work is regular. But the worst time is coming; he experiences what it is to be one of the unemployed; the loneliness, all the hopelessness and the subsequent indifference come home to him; his eyes are opened to the effect that he will never be able to derive comfort from statistics; he hears and sees things that sear the conscience as with a red-hot brand; the last evening of his exile he descends to the lowest depth, the Salvation Army shelter; that finishes him; he rushes back home, to his rooms

[1] R. Whiteing, *No. 5 John Street,* New Edition (1902), Ch. VI, p. 49.

in Piccadilly and wakes up the following morning to his familiar life.

The old life, it is like Paradise! How much easier to be good here; no noise or squalor in its quiet rooms and fragrant gardens; impossible to harbour a harsh or distracting thought here. Certainly, John Street overdid it a little in trying "to do without."

Here is Young Ridler, the perfection of finish; he is for moderation in all things, as the true secret of enjoyment; the only thing he wants is, that everything shall be "just so"; the best clothes, the best hotel, the best dinners, the best horses, and those who can 't have them, well, the beggars are used to it, they have been in training all their life.

The notes for the Report are only few; one written in John Street:

"No. 5 John Street is a sort of domestic office of the pleasaunce of Mayfair."

and another, suggested by his intercourse with the Ridlers, the rich merchant princes:

"The function of the members of this order is to suck up all the wealth of the nation into their keeping. They are as clouds — absorbed moisture for distribution in beneficent showers over the areas from which it is drawn... Thus the merchant princes to whom I refer are for ever raining back, in self-indulgence, on their fellow-creatures" [1].

It is in the height of the season and party follows party, but on the day fixed for an enormous supper he is back in John Street again; he cannot account for it, but there he is and nobody asks a question; their good breeding is perfect.

He finds his friends in high spirits about the coming Jubilee, about which they talk with incredible ignorance.

[1] R. Whiteing, *No. 5 John Street*, New Edition (1902), Ch. XX, p. 177.

Tilda is excited like a child at the approach of the holidays.

Fresh from Mayfair, he compares Tilda with the girls of his own world, who are all so very much "just so"; Tilda is 'herself in all her effects; there is no pretence in her; "she has faced the world, and fought her way in it to such poor place as she holds" [1].

Tilda treats him with great kindness, and yet with a certain aloofness; instinctively she feels that the stranger must be a being from another world, perhaps he has been a shopwalker once and she is awed by the mystery of it all. But little by little he begins to know more of her life; she is not one to squander her hard earned money on trifles or vulgar amusements; she has her own system of saving: a collection of gold wedding-rings, strung on a ribbon and carried round her neck, safely hidden by her dress. Nothing is easier in emergencies than to turn one of them into money again. He sees her life as one, free of material cares, owing to the principle: "do without", one of fortitude, helpfulness and tenderness for all that is weak, but also as one of spiritual privations.

By way of improving her mind he takes her to the National Gallery, only to find that the details of the famous productions of art appeal to her more than the whole, and that the classic music at the popular concert, makes her restless and ashamed of her want of breeding. He is more successful in the domain of literature; the effect on Tilda is the consciousness that there is something wrong with her and that she will try to be a better girl. Not bitterness or envy, or the sense of being wronged, but the yearning to rise to a higher level by her own endeavours!

His John Street friends glory in the procession, and the illumination evokes a strange awe and wonder in Tilda's

[1] R. Whiteing, *No. 5 John Street*, New Edition (1902), Ch. XXIII, p 197.

eyes. As for himself — he sees the procession as the show of the happy few, "every one of them lord of a slice of the world or its equivalents"; and he cannot help agreeing with Azrael "that a hundred men or women are spoiled and flung away, that one may be made" [1].

The most tremendous day is to be Thursday, the dinner to the Poor; Tilda has volunteered as a helper; in her view, the less eaten by those who can do without, the more there will be left for those who cannot. She has also offered to decorate her table, the children's table with flowers, and though she has parted with nearly all her wedding-rings for this purpose, she refuses all financial assistance.

It is a quiet and subdued Tilda, presiding over her table in the crowded hall, which is in reality a pathetic display of human waste.

"These are the slag of our smelting fires of civilization, yet one cannot but feel that they might as richly repay a second visitation for ore as the dross of ancient mines. They seem to demand new and nicer processes of treatment, that is all" [2]. The crowning glory of the feast will be the visit of the Princess of Wales, and Tilda is greatly agitated, when the Royal Visitor selects her table and addresses her. For a minute it seems as if Tilda's presence of mind has forsaken, her, as if the social void makes all contact impossible, but the next moment something in the girl's manner shows that she feels she has a decisive word to speak for others. Led by her first impulse she says: "Oh, Milidy, it 'ud be like the Bible, if you could come and walk down John Street Saturday nights" — but then, all at once she seems to see with the eyes of the other party, and as an afterthought the words come out: "Oh no, please Milidy, you mustn 't never come

[1] R. Whiteing, *No. 5 John Street,* New Edition (1902), Ch. XXIII, p. 197.
[2] id, Ch. XXVI, p. 230.

there — leastways Saturday nights. It 'ud only make yer want to die. Don 't give no more dinners to us grown-ups. We 're done. But make a lor about the young uns; them 's your chance" [1]. It is with a sigh and a slow, penetrating look straight into the eyes of Tilda that the Princess passes on.

With all her strength of mind Tilda is well aware that there is no way out of the old life; she has seen a shimmer of a worthier and more joyful existence, but it is not for her; after a glorious day in the country she formulates the thoughts that have troubled her since the day of the dinner to the Poor: "We in John Street can 't do no good with ourselves now. We wants picking all to pieces; and if you begin that, you'll only tear the stuff. Give the young uns a chance in their cradles, an'let the old uns die off; then you'll see a change" [2]. Soon Tilda's trouble is to be over; she finds her death in a vain attempt to prevent Azrael from blowing up the house of the Ridlers — a victim to the fatal remedy of the social disease. —

Still there is the Report to write; lying on the Malvern Hills he is aware of the presence of one who dreamed on these hills five hundred years before, a majestic, inexorable figure; under the compulsion of its gaze, he writes his Report.

He writes in a humble spirit, pressed down by a sense of responsibility and the knowledge that there is a John Street in every shining city of civilization and he gives a faithful account of his experiences and the glaring contrasts between Mayfair and John Street, and he winds up with his own meditations:

"The old mystery of regeneration is true as ever as a principle, in spite of its fantastic setting in the creeds of the hour. Democracy must get rid of the natural man, of each

[1] R Whiteing, *No. 5 John Street,* New Edition (1902), Ch. XXVI, p. 236.
[2] id, Ch. XXVIII, p. 254.

for himself, and have a new birth into the spiritual man, the ideal self of each for all.

Love, Justice, Brotherhood — only the systems are the things that have their day.

So is there no escape from the Iron Law of Brotherhood. All solutions but this have had their trial, and all have failed.

Ring out the old, ring in the new, the great moral Renaissance, the New Learning of the mind and the heart!"[1]

It is characteristic of Richard Whiteing that he ends his novel with the tragedy of human waste, and concludes his Epilogue with a note of the depression of failure, and that yet in spite of the sombre and gloomy tone, in spite of the protest against shallow optimism, and the stern, relentless realism, with which he states his facts, there is not a falling into morbid pessimism, but the admonition to believe in the great possibilities that there are in characters like that of his heroine, an appeal to our sense of responsibility, and a rousing of our activity to bring about a better future.

[1] Epilogue, pp. 283-284.

Conclusion

In this dissertation I have tried to show that the sociological novel deserves a foremost place in the realm of fiction, not in spite of, but on account of its didactic tendencies, and that the psychological element in it is a quickening power, rousing our sympathy and activity in the problems of human destiny.

We have seen that in the time discussed there is not one continued line of development, but that there are three distinct periods, each with an atmosphere of its own, impregnated with the spirit of the time:

The Period of Truth and Reason.

The Period of Organization and Co-operation.

The Period of Democracy.

It is evident that the work of the novelists, representing the feelers, is based on the philosophy of the thinkers, Rousseau, Carlyle, Ruskin, and Morris, and may inspire the work of the doers, the social workers in times to come.

In spite of the divergent tendencies in the different periods, there are still in all of them the same leading motives:

Dissatisfaction with the existing conditions.

A longing to return to Nature.

The necessity of Simplification as regards social life.

The thought that binds the three periods together, is that a world of justice, truth and love, can only be realized, when, in a spirit of brotherhood and mutual helpfulness, not bent down, but inspired by a sense of responsibility, we continue the fight against preoccupation with self, that the time may come that work shall be a pleasure and a pride and that all shall labour for the good of all.

BIBLIOGRAPHY

Bennett, E. A., 1901, Fame and Fiction.

Bjorkman, E., 1914, Voices of To-morrow.

Brandes, G., 1872-1876, Die Hauptströmungen des neunzehnten Jahrhunderts.

Brock, A. C., 1914, W. Morris.

Brun, Ch., 1910, Le Roman social en France au XIX siècle.

Brunetière, F., 1883, Le Roman naturaliste.

Cambridge History of English Literature, 1914, Vol. XI, XII, XIII.

Carlyle, Th., 1858, Chartism. Past and Present.

Cazamian, L., 1903, Le Roman social en Angleterre.

Cazamian, L., 1911, L'Angleterre moderne.

Cazamian, L., 1920, L'Evolution psychologique.

Cazamian, L., 1924, Histoire de la littérature anglaise.

Cazamian, M., 1923, Le Roman et les idées en Angleterre.

Chevalley, A., 1921, Le Roman anglais de notre temps.

Cross, W. L., 1899, The Development of the English Novel.

Cunningham, A., 1834, Biographical and critical History of the British Literature.

Dibelius, W., 1898, Englische Romankunst.

Dowden, E., 1897, The French Revolution and English Literature.

Economic Review, 1893.

Elton O., 1920, A Survey of English Literature 1830-1880.

Fabian Society, 1920, What to read.

Findlater, 1800, Liberty and Equality.

George, W. L., 1918, A novelist on Novels.

Glasier, J. B., 1920, The meaning of Socialism.

Glasier, J. B., 1921, William Morris.

Greg, W. R., 1869, Literary and Social Judgments.

Hyndman, H. M., 1902, Commercial Crises of the 19th century, 2nd edition.

Hyndman and *Morris,* 1884, A. Summary of the principles of Socialism.

Jackson, Holbrook, 1908, Great English Novelists.

Jackson, Holbrook, 1913, The Eighteen Nineties.

Jackson, Holbrook, 1908, Morris.

Lathrop, H. B., 1921, The Art of the Novelist.

Lubbock, P., 1921, The Craft of Fiction.

Locke J., 1690, Essay concerning Human Understanding.

Myers, F. W. H., 1921, Essays.

Neale, E. V., 1851, The characteristic features of some of the principal systems of Socialism.

Paine, Th., 1797, The Rights of Man.
Raleigh, W. A., 1891, The English Novel.
Ramsay Macdonald, 1911, The Socialist Movement.
Rickett, A. C., 1913, W. Morris.
Rose, J. H., 1912, The Rise of Democracy.
Rousseau, J. J., 1762, Emile.
Ruskin, J., 1862, Unto this last.
Saintsbury, G. E. B., 1912, A History of nineteenth century literature.
Saintsbury, G. E. B., 1913, The English Novel.
Speare, M. E., 1924, The Political Novel.
Stephen, Leslie, 1903, English Literature and Society in the eighteenth century.
Stephen, Leslie, 1900, The English Utilitarians.
Stoddard, F. H., 1900, The Evolution of the English Novel.
Toynbee, A., 1908, Lectures on the Industrial Revolution.
Traill, H. D., 1897, The New Fiction and other Essays on literary subjects.
Traill, H. D., 1898, Social England.
Wallace, A. R., 1903, The Wonderful Century.
Wells, H. G., 1907, Socialism and the Family.
Whiteford, R. N., 1918, Motives in English Fiction.

I

Bage, R., 1728-1801

Bage, R., 1796, Hermsprong.
Bage, R., 1792, Man as he is.

Godwin, W., 1756-1836

Brailsford, H., 1913, Shelley, Godwin and their circle.
Green, 1799, An examination of the leading principles of Political Justice.
Paul Kegan, 1876, William Godwin, 2 vol.
Simon, H., 1909, William Godwin.

Godwin, W., 1796, An Enquiry concerning Political Justice, 2nd edition.
Godwin, W., 1903, Caleb Williams (Half-forgotten books).
Godwin, W., 1796, Things as they are.

Holcroft, Th., 1745-1809

Holcroft, Th., 1792, Anna St. Ives.
Holcroft Th., 1794-1797, Hugh Trevor.

Lloyd, Ch.

Lloyd, Ch., 1798, Edmund Oliver.

Smith, Ch., 1749-1806

Smith, Ch., 1794, The Banished Man.

II

Dickens, Ch., 1812-1870

Gissing, G., 1897, Charles Dickens.
H. Jansonius, 1926. Some Aspects of Business Life.
Saunders, M. B., 1905, The philosophy of Dickens.
Weber, L., 1888, Charles Dickens.

Dickens, Ch., 1844-1848, Christmas Books.
Dickens, Ch., 1854, Hard Times.

Eliot, G., 1819-1880

Bonnell, H. H., 1902, Charlotte Bronte; George Eliot; Jane Austen: studies in their works.
Browning, O., 1892, Life of G. Eliot.
Cross, J. W., 1885, G. Eliot's Life.
Gardner, 1912, The Inner Life of G. Eliot.
Stephen, Leslie, 1902, G. Eliot.

Eliot, G., 1866, Felix Holt.

Gaskell, E. C., 1810-1865

Dullemen, J. J. v., 1924, Mrs. Gaskell.

Gaskell, E. C., 1848, Mary Barton.
Gaskell, E. C., 1855, North and South.

Kingsley, Ch., 1819-1875

Allemandy, V. H., 1910, Notes of Kingsley's Alton Locke.
Groth, E., 1893, Kingsley als Dichter und Sozialreformer.
Harrison, F., 1895, Charles Kingsley's Place in Literature.
Marriott, J. A. R., 1892, Charles Kingsley, Novelist.
Maurice, Cl., 1911, A Day with Kingsley.
Maurice, F. D., 1844, The Life of Frederick Denison Maurice.

Kingsley, Ch., 1850, Alton Locke.
Kingsley, Ch., 1851, Yeast.

Kingsley, Ch., 1908, Charles Kingsley. His Letters and Memories edited by his wife.

III

Gissing, G. R., 1857-1903

Roberts, Morley, 1912, The Private Life of Henry Maitland.
Swinnerton, F., 1912, George Gissing. A critical study.
Yates, M., 1922, George Gissing.
Young, W. T., George Gissing. (The Cambridge History of English Literature. Vol. XIII.

Gissing, G. R., 1880. WOrkers in the Dawn.
Gissing, G. R., 1886, Demos.
Gissing, G. R., 1887, Thyrza.
Gissing, G. R., 1889, The Nether World.
Gissing, G. R., 1891, New Grub Street.
Gissing, G. R., 1903, The Private Papers of Henry Ryecroft.
Gissing, G. R., 1906, The House of Cobwebs.
Gissing, G. R., 1915, Letters to an Editor.

Ward, Mrs. H., 1851-1920

Gwynn, S. L., 1915, Mrs. Humphry Ward.
Trevelyan, J. P., 1923, The Life of Mrs. Humphy Ward.
Walters, J. S., 1912, Mrs. Humphry Ward.

Ward, Mrs. H., 1894, Marcella.
Ward, Mrs. H., 1896, Sir George Tressady.

Morrison, A., 1863

Morrison, A., 1894, Tales of Mean Streets.
Morrison, A., 1896, A Child of the Jago.
Morrison, A., 1899, To London Town.

White, W. H., 1831-1913

Nicoll, Sir William R., 1924, Memories of Mark Rutherford.
Rutherford, M., 1889, Autobiography.
Taylor, A. E., 1914, The Novels of Mark Rutherford.
White W. H., 1913, The early Life of Mark Rutherford.

Rutherford, M., 1923, The Novels of Mark Rutherford, 6 volumes.
Rutherford, M., 1887, The Revolution in Tanner's Lane.
White, W. H., 1924, Letters to three Friends.

Whiteing, R., 1840

Whiteing, R., 1867, Mr. Sprouts, his opinions.
Whiteing, R., 1888, The Island.
Whiteing, R., 1899, No. 5 John Street.
Whiteing, R., 1915, My Harvest.

I

The didactic element enhances the value of the sociological novel.

II

Godwin's *Caleb Williams* is a study of character rather than the prototype of the detective novel.

III

Madeleine Cazamian misunderstands Gissing in saying: „Nous sommes ici près du pessimisme absolu, tel qu'il s'exprime, tel qu'on l'étudiera dans l'œuvre de Hardy, et surtout dans celle de Gissing."

M. L. Cazamian, *Le Roman et les Idées en Angleterre,* Ch. IV, p. 295.

IV

W. L. Cross wrongly asserts that the purpose of Aphra Behn's *Oroonoko* was, to awaken Christendom to the horrors of slavery.

W. L. Cross, *The Development of the English novel,* Ch. I, p. 20.

V

W. H. Fleming idealizes Shylock's daughter in the comparison:

"A delicate plant in a dark cave struggles toward the ray of light which shines through a fissure of the rock."

W. H. Fleming, *Shakespeare's Plots,* Ch. IV, pp. 182, 183.

VI

To prove that Shakespeare is for all times it is not necessary to produce Hamlet in modern clothes.

VII

The buttonholing method of George Eliot is not a drawback.

VIII

The text of the 1st Folio of Beaumont and Fletcher's *Love's Pilgrimage,* Act I: Scene 1, ll. 25-28.

"Gossip, I have found

The root of all; kneel, pray, it is thyself
Art cause thereof: each person is the Founder
Of his own fortune, good or bad."

is to be preferred to the text of the 2nd Folio, which omits the word: "pray".

IX

The advocates of the Simplified Spelling of the English Language, though appealing to common sense, commit the error of leaving out of account the aspect of the written word.

Cf. *An appeal to Common Sense* isyud bi the Simplifyd Speling Sosyeti 44. Great Rusell Street London. W.C.

X

De voorstelling, dat werkwoorden alleen transitief genoemd kunnen worden, als zij conversie in het passivum toelaten, is onjuist.

XI

Het is te betreuren, dat de vreemde talen te weinig gesproken worden op onze Hogere Burgerscholen.

XII

Bij het onderwijs in de vreemde talen is het van meer belang, dat de leerlingen de stemming van een gedicht voelen, en de karakters van een drama begrijpen, dan dat zij de woorden ervan kunnen vertalen.